THE ART OF HORIZON ZERO DAWN
ISBN: 9781785653636
Limited Edition ISBN: 9781785653711

Published by Titan Books
A division of Titan Publishing Group Ltd.
144 Southwark St.
London
SE1 0UP

First edition: February 2017
10 9 8 7 6 5

Horizon Zero Dawn™ ©2017 Sony Interactive
Entertainment Europe. Published by Sony Interactive
Entertainment Europe. Developed by Guerrilla.
"Horizon Zero Dawn" is a trademark of Sony Interactive
Entertainment Europe. All rights reserved.

To receive advance information, news, competitions, and exclusive offers online, please sign up for the Titan newsletter on our website: www.titanbooks.com

Did you enjoy this book? We love to hear from our readers. Please e-mail us at: readerfeedback@titanemail.com or write to Reader Feedback at the above address.

A CIP catalogue record for this title is available from the British Library.

Printed and bound in China.

THE ART OF
HORIZON
ZERO DAWN

PAUL DAVIES

TITAN BOOKS

CONTENTS

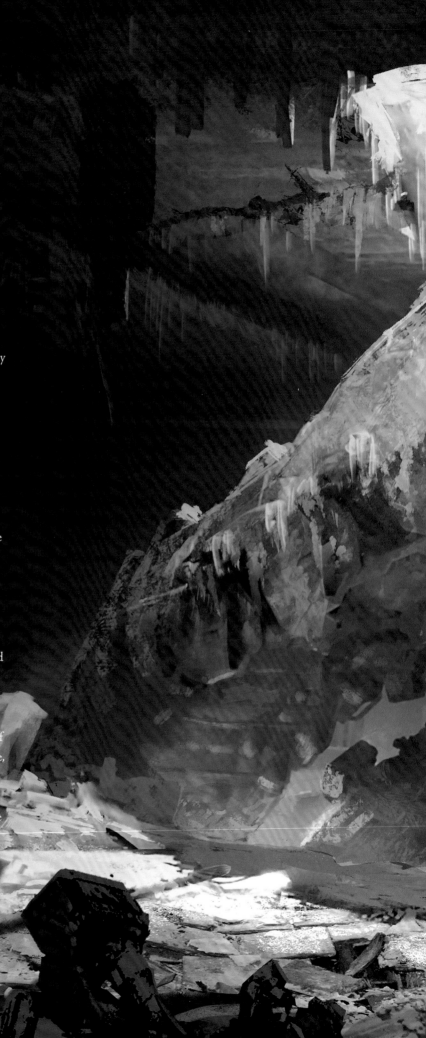

FOREWORD

BY ROLAND IJZERMANS

Being a concept artist is somewhat like being an explorer.

When Guerrilla officially started development on *Horizon Zero Dawn* in 2010, a tangible sense of wonder and excitement came over our visual design department. It was as though we'd embarked on an expedition into unknown territory, meticulously charting and giving visual expression to everything we encountered along the way.

From the outset, we wanted to make sure that we did justice to *Horizon Zero Dawn*'s unique vision for a post-post-apocalyptic future. Our concept designs had to feel like they belonged in that future, so we performed a great deal of research on what its environments, inhabitants, cultures and surviving technology would look like, how they would interact, and how they could've evolved over time.

At the same time, we wanted to cover as much ground as possible – to make *Horizon Zero Dawn* as big and varied as we possibly could. The volume of artwork required to accomplish that goal was beyond anything our visual design department had ever handled before, and it took an enormous effort by a very large group of artists (both internally and externally) to pull off.

In spite of such challenges, our visual exploration of the world of *Horizon Zero Dawn* has been a tremendously rewarding exercise, and the selection of artworks presented in this book serves as a testament to the dedication, skill and talent of every concept artist who took the journey with us. We hope it will give you the same sense of wonder and excitement that we felt along the way.

Thank you,

ROLAND IJZERMANS, ASSISTANT ART DIRECTOR

NORA

To appreciate even a little about Aloy, the lead protagonist of *Horizon Zero Dawn*, we must first know something of her tribe. The Nora are reclusive hunter-gatherers whose territory covers portions of the present-day Colorado Rockies, now seen as their Sacred Land. Surrounded by natural beauty, the tribe is a matriarchal society following a religion based on the worship of motherhood and child-rearing. Their culture is built upon a fierce hunter-warrior ethic that puts food on the table and protects their villages; the largest of which is Mother's Heart. They hunt animals and machines alike.

While the Nora are led by a council of female Matriarchs, both women and men fulfil the role of 'brave', guarding tribal lands and hunting the many machine species. The Nora often use deadly force to drive intruders from their land. No other tribe in *Horizon Zero Dawn* matches their skill in archery or exceeds their ability to track quarry.

Nora legend holds that the ruins of the ancient 'Metal World' are tainted and corrupted by the avarice of their long-dead inhabitants. To explore these ancient ruins is to break the most sacred of taboos. Those who do risk permanent exile.

⬡ ALOY

From the earliest days of the *Horizon Zero Dawn* project, Guerrilla knew that Aloy would always be of the world but also somewhat separate. The character and design of Aloy evolved over time, but stayed true to the core concept influenced by the story of David and Goliath: the player cleverly hunts the machines, rather than using brute force. Early concept paintings portrayed gigantic, ferocious machines contrasting with a tiny figure in the foreground.

From here on in, Guerrilla created a character who was skilled, smart, strategic and agile, to guide the player to this playstyle. Players would grow into this identity, rather than simply directing an avatar. Even though they would have choice through conversation options and playstyle, their options would always consist of things that Aloy could or would do.

Dan Calvert, Art-Director (Characters): "From its earliest beginnings, *Horizon Zero Dawn* pivoted around three core concepts: animalistic machines, an open world of natural beauty, and the defiant red-headed girl who makes her place in this land. Developing Aloy's visual ID was one of our first priorities, and her final look was key to the visual development of the rest of the cast."

Guerrilla's concept team toyed with the idea of making Aloy a younger girl, as seen in these images, before deciding that a more mature character would create better narrative opportunities. Her deadly grace is captured with flowing hair and wind-blown furs.

Earlier concepts used a looser, more illustrative and expressive style to explore Aloy's personality and expressions. Gradually this was honed to achieve realism and believability.

Aloy is motherless in a tribe that worships motherhood, and so she is considered an outcast. Her guardian, however, raised her in the Nora traditions, teaching her to adopt their crafting and hunting techniques. Given her outsider's perspective, Aloy invents new ways of doing and making things. She has an individualistic streak that is expressed in her unique appearance, even when clothed in tribal garb. Her outfits are designed purely for agility and protection; no heavy plate armor, just practical hunting gear that speaks to her personality. From a concept point of view, the outfits include lots of iconography and decorations designed to accentuate graceful movement. Color choices are vibrant, with flowing surfaces and loose hanging items for abundant secondary motion.

Guerrilla Games' artists took some liberties with the literal practicality of the costumes, but great effort was spent ensuring that the construction of the costume was believable and consistent.

"These are just a small selection of the experimental illustrations used to develop Aloy's hair. Guerrilla carefully considered how the shape and motion of the hair, combined with gestures and visage, could be used to accentuate Aloy's expressiveness." Ilya Golitsyn, Senior Concept Artist

Aloy's hair became increasingly important over time, as Guerrilla aimed for it to be a part of her character. It was a design challenge to make the amount of hair work on the in-game character model due to the way it flows and creates additional volume. The vibrant color was chosen because it helped differentiate her from other characters in her tribe, setting her apart as an individual.

While her costume designs incorporate materials and shapes linked to different tribes, her hair is always distinct and easily recognizable. Ilya Golitsyn, Senior Concept Artist, explains: "We wanted to ensure that Aloy would be immediately identifiable, regardless of what she was wearing, so her hair became a key motif that remained consistent across all of her outfits."

DREADLOCK MOHAWK

DREADLOCK MOHAWK // DARK

TEASED HAIR W/ BANDANA

"CORN ROWS"

A great deal of thought has been given to Aloy's personality and philosophy, which in turn influences how she looks and behaves. The Nora have formed their own beliefs regarding the fate of the world and how the machines came to be. Aloy's sharp insight and rational mind, compounded with her outsider status, often pulls her into conflict with those who hold such beliefs.

"While drawing Aloy, I focused on using rich, earthy tones that reflect her connection with nature and intuitive approach to life. However, I felt it was important to balance these tones with details and accents that have a double function: adding to the handmade feel of her accessories, as well as alluding to the availability of machine parts and machinery that can be scavenged and used as decoration.

I was lucky to be able to do a lot of work on her hair, which was a fun challenge. The goal was to keep a sense of volume and richness, without making the hair look unrealistically glossy or clean for a huntress who lives in the harsh wilderness. The most important thing for me was that my sketches of Aloy convey a strong sense of personality - she's a character of her own, not just a character design." Lois van Baarle, Freelance Concept Artist.

LEFT AND ABOVE: These sketches were among those used to develop Aloy's expressiveness and emotional range, from relaxed and charming, to fierce and focused, through to thoughtful and pensive.

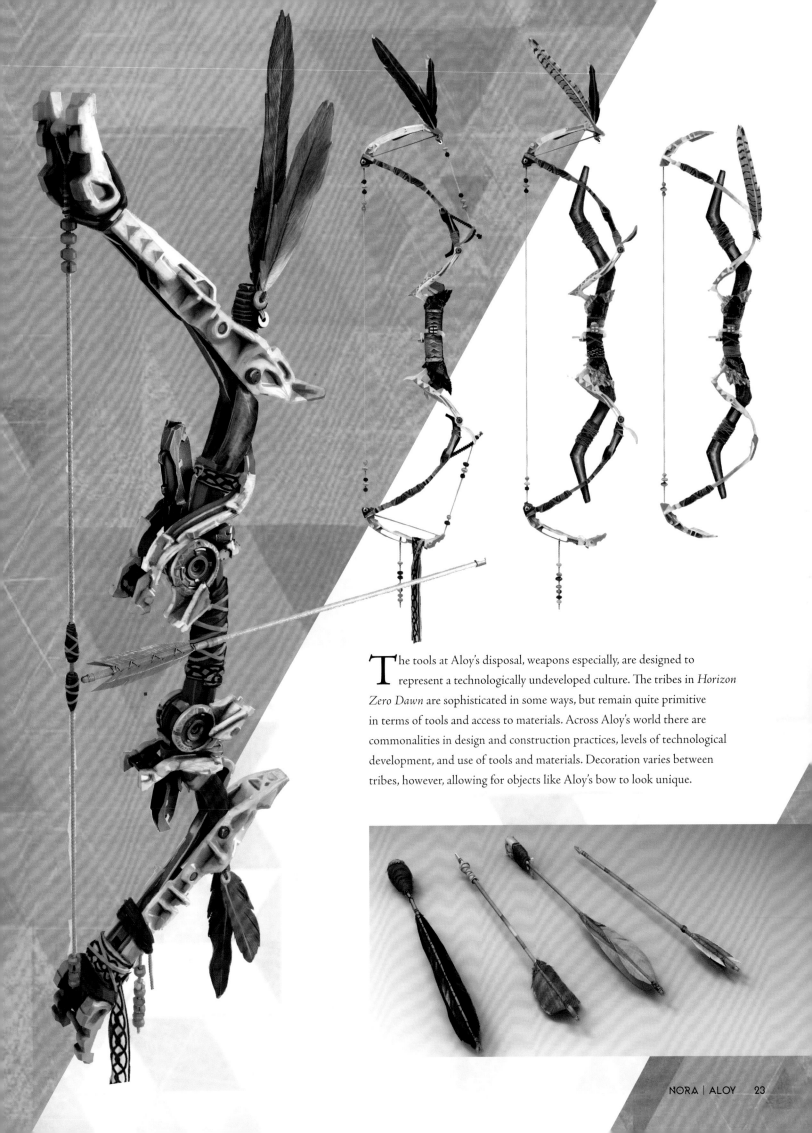

The tools at Aloy's disposal, weapons especially, are designed to represent a technologically undeveloped culture. The tribes in *Horizon Zero Dawn* are sophisticated in some ways, but remain quite primitive in terms of tools and access to materials. Across Aloy's world there are commonalities in design and construction practices, levels of technological development, and use of tools and materials. Decoration varies between tribes, however, allowing for objects like Aloy's bow to look unique.

As Aloy is an outsider, with no fixed place in any tribe, it makes sense for her to customize her look as she moves through the world of *Horizon Zero Dawn*. Her wide range of costumes not only has a gameplay function, with each one providing unique abilities when worn, but also helps foster an understanding of Aloy as a character. Although every outfit is unique and representative of a tribe, there is still a distinct silhouette that preserves Aloy's visual identity. It includes repeating elements such as the skirts and bags, along with motifs that are uniquely 'Aloy', such as her hair.

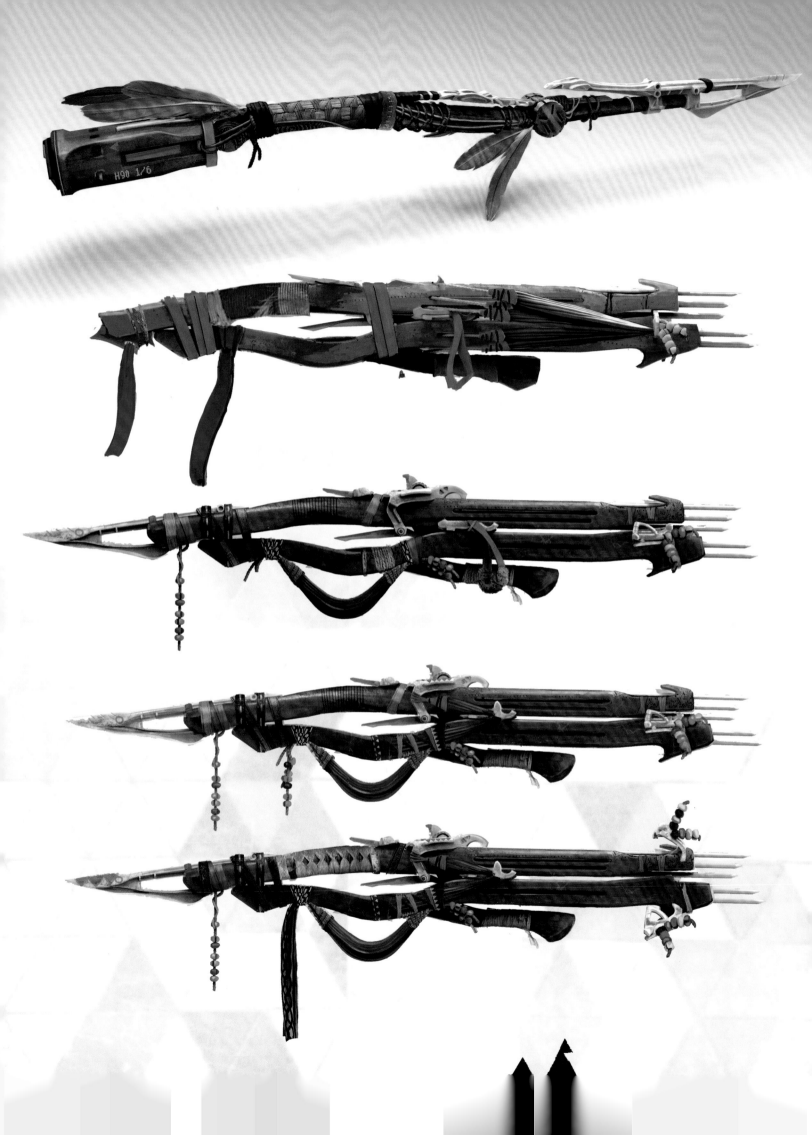

With authenticity among the key design principles, the weapons in *Horizon Zero Dawn* needed to look and operate in a believable fashion. The fun part for Guerrilla was to imagine how humans might go about constructing them, given that each tribe only has a limited level of technological understanding. For each weapon, the artists dreamed up designs that had not been done before. Some have a strategic one-off purpose, such as those blasted from the machines during battle. Smaller bits and pieces, though, can be used to build and craft a better armory.

Weapon construction among the tribes is largely down to trial and error. Nobody knows for sure how the various parts will interact, but by clicking things together and relying on a bit of luck, the next 'sonic blaster' might emerge.

CHARACTERS

In the matriarchal Nora society, women are valued higher than men for their physical and intellectual flexibility. The Nora believe a women's even temperament makes her better suited to be a leader, one that's more conducive to long-term stability. Hence, the most splendid character is the elderly Matriarch, a grandmother worthy of the greatest honor. Matriarchs not only take care of their own bloodline, but manage the welfare of their settlement as a whole – 'super mothers'.

A woman's capability to create new life has greatly inspired Nora spiritual sensibility, resulting in the worship of an 'All-Mother' deity. Beyond the ruling circle of High Matriarchs, leadership positions are almost always held by women, including martial leaders such as the War-Chief. Since the Nora are a devout and spiritual people, they do not dress exclusively in practical garb, but adorn their clothes with iconography and trinkets designed to bestow the blessing and favor of the All-Mother.

LEFT: "Each tribe has a different relationship with the machines. The Nora see them as little more than a resource, provided as a blessing from All-Mother. They hunt machines for parts which they then use to create armor, weapons and tools. Given the risks involved, machine-derived equipment is treasured by the owner, and used as a show of status and hunting aptitude." Ilya Golitsyn

LOCATIONS

The present-day Rocky Mountain National Park, Colorado, is considered to be among the most beatific locations on earth. In *Horizon Zero Dawn*, the Rockies are an ancestral home to the Nora tribe. Their settlements are easy to defend with close proximity to mountain passes, guarded by watchtowers in the approach. Most Nora take shelter in wooden lodges within the settlements, safely away from the machines roaming outside. machines are treated as a blessing from the All-Mother, but the Nora also understand their danger and take no unnecessary risks. As a further precaution, Nora habitats are built on mountain slopes instead of the lower ground. On this page, a typical Nora settlement can be seen.

Among the tribes that feature in *Horizon Zero Dawn*, the Nora are the most balanced and secure. Nora culture is generally communal. Hunters share their kills, and gatherers their harvest, with the entire settlement. Their villages are well defended against intruders, but their purpose is otherwise to shelter one generation after the next. There is a sensible, sometimes delightful, reason for everything and this begins with their village sites. Many are in the proximity to an ancestral ground, which is chosen for its natural beauty: on top of a tall ridge, near a little waterfall, or on the rock peninsula of a mountain lake.

Most Nora live in communal lodges. Braves hunt for food, escort gathering parties, and patrol tribal lands, driving off or killing trespassers. Gatherers forage for nuts, berries, edible roots, and usable plants, and also practice "forest gardening" to increase food and fiber output.

BELOW: Monotone concepts are used to describe the contours and general layouts of areas, setting the mood while sketching out gameplay challenges for artists and game designers to follow. Important, characteristic elements such as watchtowers and torches are highlighted. These may also be used to storyboard progression through missions or specific set-pieces, showing the scene from all angles while providing a sense of scale.

This impressive gateway [right] is covered in Nora symbolism – in this case signs representing their goddess, the All-Mother. It leads to a sheltered area called the Embrace, where the Nora train their young hunters and raise their children. The Nora are very protective of their own people, building massive fortifications around settlements; enormous walls on the frontiers of Nora territory. They are quite xenophobic, expressed through their suspicion toward outlanders. Indeed, prior to events in *Horizon Zero Dawn*, it was forbidden for anyone other than Nora to enter their territory; intruders would be killed on sight. To the left of the main image, the interior is a sacred location. However, the Nora do not gather at designated buildings to worship the All-Mother, choosing to express their beliefs during their day-to-day lives instead.

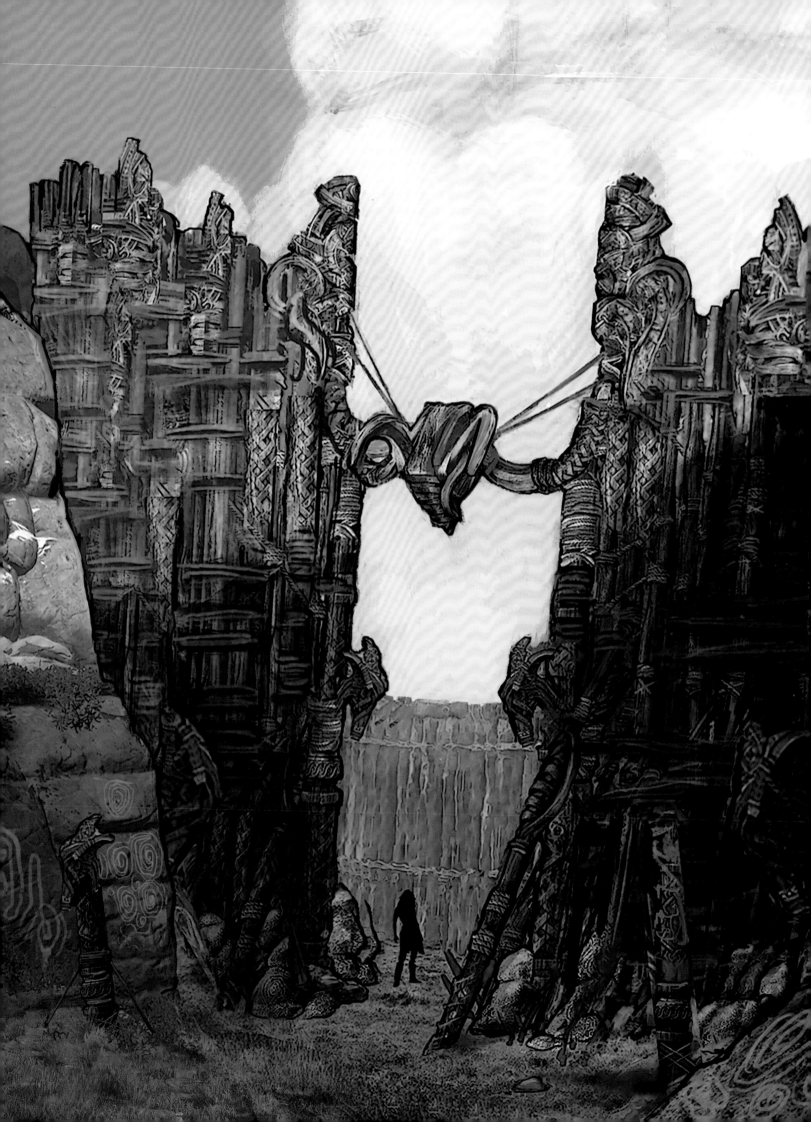

This is a typical house found within a Nora settlement, using aspen wood for the outhouse, debarked trunks for the main walls, decoratively rope-knotted connections and very distinctive curvature of the roof. Above the entrance is an assembly of salvaged machine parts, and behind that wooden roof shingles. The chimney is made out of wood and clay. The foundations are laid with rock. It is a practical design.

CULTURE

This spellbinding scene is an early concept of a Nora ceremony called 'The Proving'. Nora ceremonies are used to recognize the seasons and the major cycles of machine behavior, as well as to celebrate the miracle of childbirth. Every birthday is a significant event, although celebrating the blessed mother as opposed to their fortunate offspring. The children bring gifts to their mothers, not the other way around, spending the entire day together. If the mother has passed, the child spends all day beside her grave. There are rituals held before every hunt, with blessings made and codes of proper behavior observed.

'The Proving,' is the most significant Nora ritual, held every year, in which youth compete to be recognized as adult Nora. To pass the test is moderately challenging, but to win the contest is very difficult indeed. Every year, The Proving's winner is given a special audience with the Matriarchs and is allowed to make a special request, such as an immediate mate-blessing or a bow crafted by a master bowyer. So long as the winner's request is reasonable, the Matriarchs will grant it.

"Making "the Proving" was an interesting chance to explore how the Nora approach ceremony. I wanted it to feel tranquil, like the quiet before the storm, but still have enough going on to show that it is also a celebration."
Eric Felten, Concept Artist

LEFT: "The birth channel of All-Mother, a steel-ribbed tunnel that leads to the womb of the mountain. Only Matriarchs may pass the threshold of the tunnel. Within lies a large chamber that the Matriarchs regard as a sacred place, and use for monthly gatherings." Ilya Golitsyn

ABOVE AND TOP LEFT: "The All-Mother mountain is the Nora tribe's most sacred place of all. They believe it is the birthplace of life itself. I really wanted to emphasize the importance of this entrance into the All-Mother by making it a huge and complex structure; with totems, candles, and offerings to their goddess." Eric Felten

BELOW: Nora symbolism revolves around the worship of the All-Mother – so the tribal patterns that adorn these items are reminiscent of female anatomy, particularly the life-giving womb. Each item on the page is carefully designed by the Guerrilla team, showing a meticulous attention to detail when building believable and distinct cultures.

Nora craft is somewhat primitive, with the technologies available to the tribe somewhere around Bronze Age levels. The base material for any construction is wood, which carpenters will neatly prepare by debarking and (usually) shaving to size and shape. The Nora are also skillful leatherworkers, incorporating hide into their everyday items in both practical and decorative ways. Though their technology is primitive compared to the likes of the Oseram and Carja tribes, the Nora have a sophisticated culture, with an emphasis on spirituality. They make practical items that can weather the rugged terrain of their home but also incorporate religious symbolism, so that they may honor the All-Mother in their everyday life.

CARJA

Among all the tribes of *Horizon Zero Dawn*, the Carja Sundom boasts the most advanced culture. Using the advantages of their geographical position, the Carja have developed agriculture and trade while other tribes still rely on hunting and gathering. The Carja's impregnable capital, Meridian, provides security for a civilized population. Artisans and traders flourish here, serving sophisticated, well-to-do citizens. Carja civilization towers over the other tribes, just as the Sun of their religion rises above the horizon of their mesa valley.

Such ascendance cannot go on forever, and the Carja Sundom faces a decline. The increased aggression of the machines threatens the borders of Carja territory, disrupting agriculture and trade. In addition, the growing influence of the Oseram tribe threatens Meridian's trade dominance. As a result of the inability of the Carja's ruling Sun-King to deal with these challenges, a power struggle has erupted, escalating into all-out civil war. It has split the tribe into two: the winning side, the Sun Carja, has kept Meridian, while the losing side, known as the Shadow Carja, has been banished, finding refuge in the heavily-militarized Sunfall.

☿ CHARACTERS

Tradition meets the latest fashion in Meridian clothing and accessories, as varied as the Sun Carja people's ethnic and cultural backgrounds. "Extensive trade and the efforts of the Hunters Lodge provide Meridian tailors access to a variety of exotic materials and rare machine dyes," informs Ilya Golitsyn. "Consequently, the garb of the Carja is the most refined and elaborate in the world; a riot of colors. Through ages of perfecting the techniques of machine plate-working, the Carja have developed the most sophisticated ways to apply the materials of mechanical fauna. While more primitive tribes would roughly affix more or less useful machine parts on their garments, Meridian artisans interweave fine fitted machine elements into comfortable and functional pieces."

"Among the most pivotal elements of Carja iconography is the avian motif, taking its influence from the location that they live in, with its tall rocks and prevalent winds, as well as its birds, both machine and natural, that ride the currents. Many garments are decorated with feathers or flowing silk ribbons." Ilya Golitsyn

Machine hunting is a most dangerous and complex task
for humans. Which is why machine hunters, or outlanders,
are so revered in almost every tribe. For Carja outlanders,
machine hunting is much more. In such a developed culture,
killing machines is not only a means of survival, but an art
form – a show and a ritual.

"While designing machine hunters for the Carja tribe,
I wanted their way of hunting to reflect the vanity and
decadence of a sophisticated culture. These flamboyant
acrobats are showmen that hunt for fame and fortune, and
not so much for prey." Ilya Golitsyn

As the only highly civilized culture, the Carja is also the tribe that has the most developed social hierarchy. At the top stands the Sun-King, ruler of the Carja and living incarnation of the sun. Below him are the Priests, who observe the sun and stars, cast auguries, manage the treasury, and serve as magistrates to decide conflicts among Carja of lesser rank. Next come the Nobles, typically traders or military officers. Each noble belongs to a family house. Distinguished nobles serve as commanders or provincial governors at Carja outposts. Most of the tribe's fighting men took the side of the insurgency to become Shadow Carja, and so the Meridian military now mainly comprises of city guards and Oseram mercenaries. Beneath them are Artisans, Traders, and Merchants. Finally, the lowest class belongs to Laborers: farmers, porters, and servants.

OPPOSITE: "Behold Avad, son of Jahadin, heir to Araman, the fourteenth Sun-King, first of his name. High atop Meridian's mesa, from his golden throne in the Palace of the Sun, he governs the Carja Sundom."
Ilya Golitsyn

☿ LOCATIONS

'Immense' is the word that best describes Meridian's enviable location, as well as the architecture found within its walls. Its territory extends to both sides of the Colorado River, absorbing the present-day Monument Valley, now overrun with teeming jungle growth. Inside the city, visitors are treated to some of the most sophisticated examples of architecture that exists in their pleasant post-apocalyptic world. Owing to its central location, trade has influenced Meridian's construction methods and building forms. Rooftops touch the sky, with richer households boasting balconies and pavilions.

Outside the gates, the surrounding lands are rich in vegetation after climate change, though the famous cliffs and gorges of the canyon are still visible. Meridian is the center of culture in the known world, possessing every thinkable town facility, including shops, pubs, restaurants, crafters, musicians and guilds. On its streets Aloy encounters a wide range of individuals: town criers, beggars, bards, children, gamblers and representatives from other tribes. Meridian also includes unique facilities like the Palace of the Sun, the old Sun Ring, the Hunters Lodge, and expansive farmlands and fortifications.

The oldest types of settlement in the Meridian valley are these cliff villages, built at a time when machine herds roamed the land and no defensive wall was strong enough to hold them back. Gradually, as the land became safer, the dwelling places spread to lower ground.

When it became safe for the people to settle in the valleys and near the riverbeds, conditions for farming and trade vastly improved. Places such as this used the rivers for commercial transportation, leading to rapid cultural growth. Lighter, lower-ground settlements began to characterize the region, although the architecture is still based on the cave-like structures from centuries past. Also, verandas and balconies are far more common now. In general, the Carja villages give an impression of prosperity and calm; with its ideal climate and generous culture, life isn't bad at all.

BELOW: Balconies, said to be characteristic of the region, are worked into various iterations to see how they might belong in a typical Meridian quarter. The architects pay little or no mind to the effects of gravity, with turrets and towers atop turrets and towers, and dainty verandas sandwiched in between.

Meridian is exciting in part because of its density, and the sensation of being dwarfed by its highest peaks. The city is imposing in this respect; the traders that pass through are merely in servitude to all its grandeur, like actors treading onto an elaborately presented stage. These concepts clearly show the contrast between the more affluent quarters [left] and the underprivileged areas [below]. However, in the way everything is presented, the quality of life does not seem too far apart between the two. In the wealthier buildings, tropical vegetation can be seen twisting around the pillars and bulging from the balconies. In the shadows of the poorer alleyways the walls are completely bare, revealing construction methods. The basics consist of local rocks and hewn blocks, sometimes covered in plaster.

LEFT: Traders converse in the shade, perhaps sharing philosophical views in addition to comparing the prices of goods. Under the rule of the new Sun-King, cultural exchange in Meridian has become every bit as important to its development as the wealth that it has acquired.

"The headquarters of the Hunters Lodge, an impressive structure befitting one of the most powerful organizations in the world. As the main hub for all outlanders who roam the wilderness hunting dangerous and rare machines, it is appropriate for the Hunters Lodge to be located in Meridian, center of the known world's trade. Here, successful hunters boast their trophies, adventurers come for dangerous contracts, and traders make deals on precious machine resources." Ilya Golitsyn

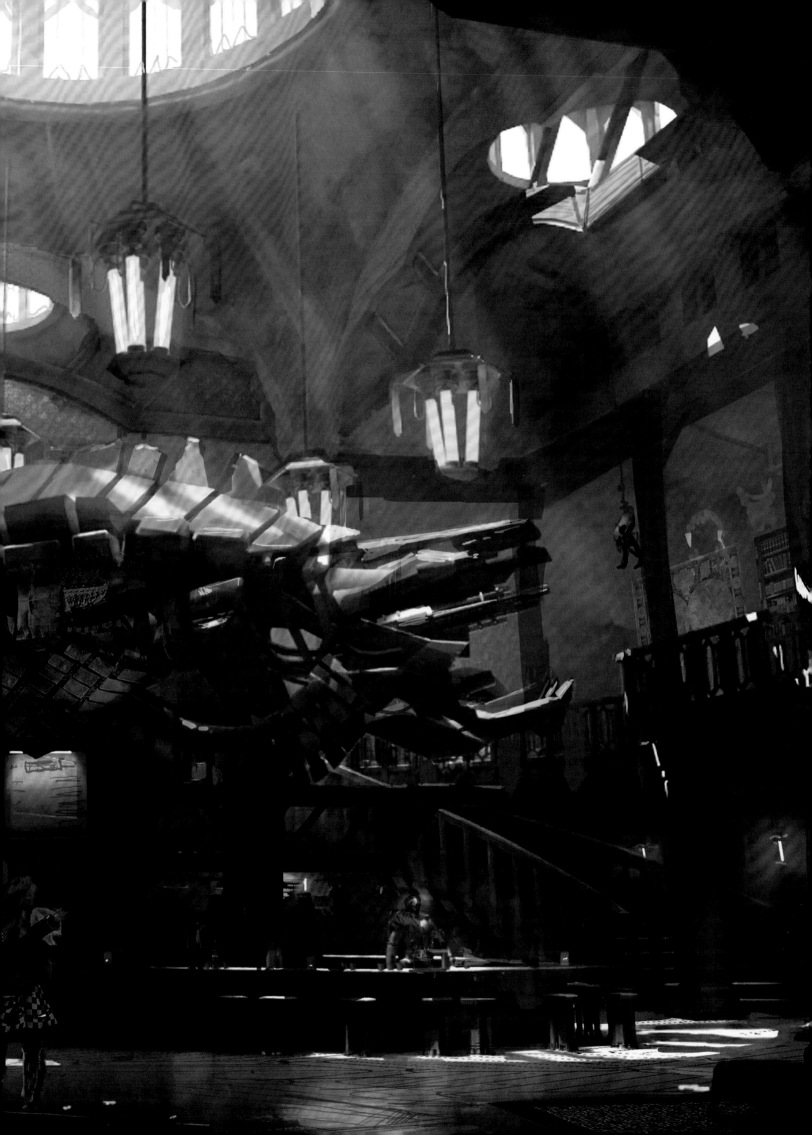

☿ CULTURE

The Carja worship the Sun as a life-giving deity, and believe the Sun-King is its human incarnation. The Carja calendar is organized around the solstices and equinoxes. Massive festivals are held four times a year. In the darker past, when a harvest failed or other crises emerged, slaves or captives were slaughtered in the Sun Ring during these holidays, sacrificed to bring back the favor of the Sun. Later, these rituals evolved into theatrical performances and gladiatorial games.

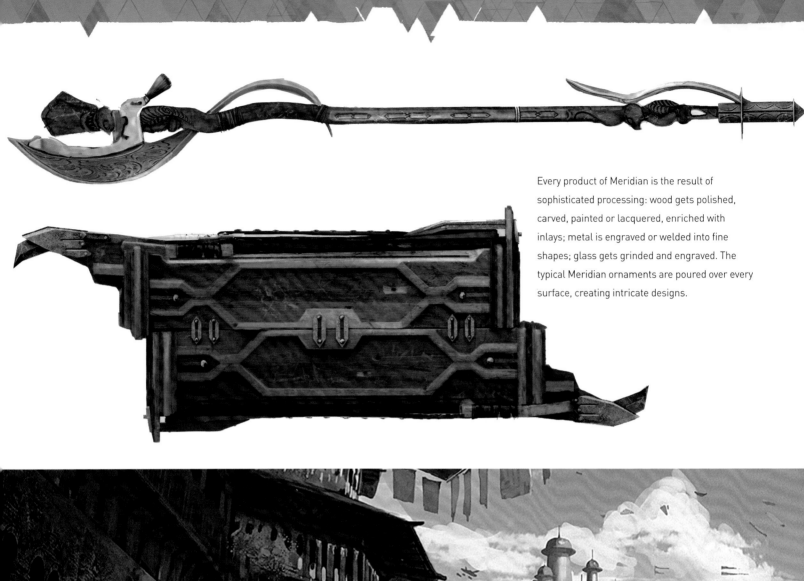

Every product of Meridian is the result of sophisticated processing: wood gets polished, carved, painted or lacquered, enriched with inlays; metal is engraved or welded into fine shapes; glass gets grinded and engraved. The typical Meridian ornaments are poured over every surface, creating intricate designs.

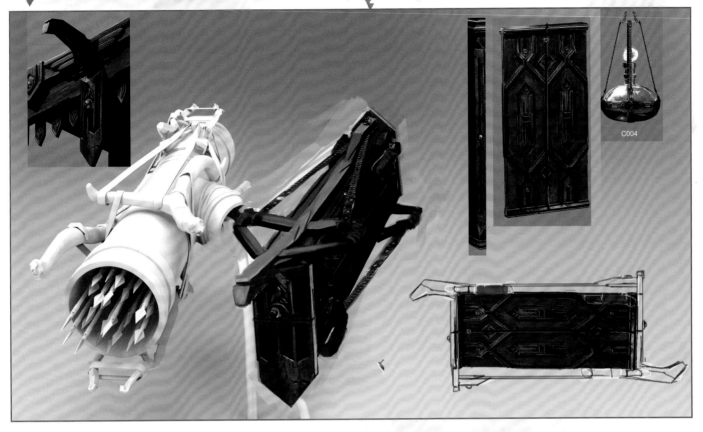

C004

Composed of stylized machine feathers, the star with eight rays (occasionally seen with four or five rays) is a representation of the Sun god of the Carja religion. It can be found everywhere in Meridian, from pavement mosaics and door ornamentation to the High Priest's gowns and the Sun-King's symbols of power.

☿ SHADOW CARJA

The exiles of the Carja civil war, the hardline Shadow Carja, mainly consist of the deposed Sun-King's military, priests, and old aristocracy. Itamen, the young son of the late king, is held captive by the Shadow Carja, who use him as a figurehead. They have taken refuge in the summer residence of the Carja kings, Sunfall, an imposing fortification now surrounded by rugged refugee camps. One of the key locations found within Sunfall is a second Sun Ring, a huge arena for gladiatorial games and religious rituals. When the Mad Sun-King invoked brutal religious rituals from the distant past, thousands of captives and dissenters were forced to battle machines to the death in ritual combat inside the Sun Ring.

Here we see Itamen, son of the overthrown mad king Jahadin, and his mother, the dowager queen Nasadi, both pawns in Helis and Bahavas's dangerous game. They preside over the Shadow Carja who, having been driven from their ancestral lands, now cling fervently to tradition. Shadow Carja iconography is aggressive, especially when it comes to armor and military uniforms. Dress varies wildly with class: the military and elites have access to fine or exotic materials through raiding and hoarding, but such access pales in comparison to their cousins in Meridian, so their dress remains relatively austere. Priests still employ ornamentation, but in a far less ostentatious way than that of the Sun Carja.

Shadow Carja soldiers consider themselves the unbroken continuation of ancient Carja military tradition. Their organization, uniforms and equipment are inherited from the historical doctrine of the Sundom. Carja military is divided into two sub-classes: Kestrels, elite warriors who wear feathered uniforms, and rank-and-file Soldiers. Most of them have followed their general, Helis, into insurgency.

LEFT: Vanasha is a handmaiden to Dowager Queen Nasadi, mother to the pretender Sun-King Itamen.

"As the pinnacle of craftsmanship in the *Horizon Zero Dawn* world, Carja armor had to look the most advanced, without using any forged metal. We decided to show it through more sophisticated ways of armor construction. Small scales of machine plating are cut and polished in order to perfectly fit into complex constructions, which give sufficient protection while remaining quite flexible." Ilya Golitsyn

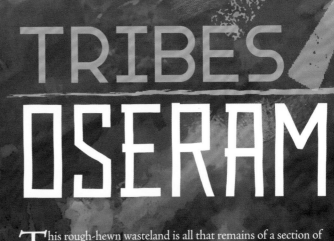

TRIBES
OSERAM

This rough-hewn wasteland is all that remains of a section of coniferous forest on the outskirts of an Oseram village. The Oseram devour entire landscapes, gathering large quantities of fuel for foundries and smithies that produce fine metal items of all kinds. Oseram people are the most technologically advanced in *Horizon Zero Dawn*, and the only tribe to work in iron.

The main concept for the Oseram is one of ruggedness and function over form, although this isn't to say that their output is without creative thought. While the households and work areas are simple, mortar-less stone affairs, the inhabitants are elaborately dressed. Furniture, accessories and tools are likewise skillfully fashioned, ranging from practical wood-mounted braziers to embossed and carefully tuned ceremonial gongs. Although devastating, the Oseram treatment of the land and its resources is efficient – expertly finished and mindful of diminishing supplies. Oseram culture can be defined by pride of practice and the tendency to reinforce with metal, even if it's not always essential.

CHARACTERS

The Oseram Vanguard are a member of the elite military force that helped Sun-King Avad win the civil war and capture Meridian. They are exceptional smiths, trappers and traders. The Oseram are hardy and burly people, and strong-willed whether large or slender. While women are said to be as influential as the men in general leadership, overall Oseram government is male-dominated; women are welcomed and heard during debate, but their place is considered to be in the village, while men handle hunting, excavation and trade.

"The biggest challenge in designing Oseram armor was to have them use a lot of forged metal elements, without making it look too much like typical medieval armor. We ended up using more primitive ways to connect rough metal pieces to a leather base, more knots and ropes rather than buckles and chain mail."
Ilya Golitsyn

Oseram armor derives from their blacksmithing roots. Warriors first wore leather smocks into battle. Over time, work robes were reinforced: aprons turned into cuirasses, smelting masks into helmets, blacksmithing gloves into spiked gauntlets.

LOCATIONS

Oseram architecture marries stone with wood, and welds it together with metal anchors. The most common of all structures is the beehive hut, but its usage has shifted from residential to storage due to aging design. Oseram villages are predominantly made up of central domed buildings, with outbuildings used for baking and larders. Houses are often built into the slopes of hills, so that the terrace of one home might become another's front yard. As more houses are built, the number of interconnecting staircases organically increases. Modern Oseram architecture now integrates some outbuildings, plastering on chimneys where needed, and patios for decoration. With no mortar used, the weight of the material and strength of the binding keeps things upright. Wood is considered to be a weak material, greatly improved by adding metal.

Oseram villages are remarkable for their lack of grandeur. Even those that have existed for hundreds of years retain the rustic look of frontier outposts and forts. Rugged exteriors reflect values of functionality over ostentation. Villages are independent political entities with clearly defined territorial holdings. In theory they would come to each other's defense when attacked by an external enemy, but in practice the impregnability of the villages has rendered this a moot point.

A   B   C   D

One can clearly see the variety of Oseram architecture and crafting capability by contrasting the beehive hut [above], used as temporary housing around logging sites, with the impressive Clan Mansion [left]. The latter's balustrade framing the roof terrace, long flights of steps, food storage facilities and copper-encased chimneys make it seem more like a castle than an abode. Again we see the metal bindings and a distinctive domed theme. Every last ounce of local resource has been stacked, strapped and riveted to rise out of the rock.

BELOW: This series of diagrams shows how an Oseram charcoal stack is constructed using the help of machines and pulleys. It comprises one or two central trees placed as a spine, logs to serve as steps to reach the top of the pile, and grass sods covering the whole thing.

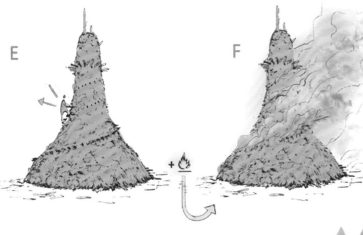

E   F   G   H

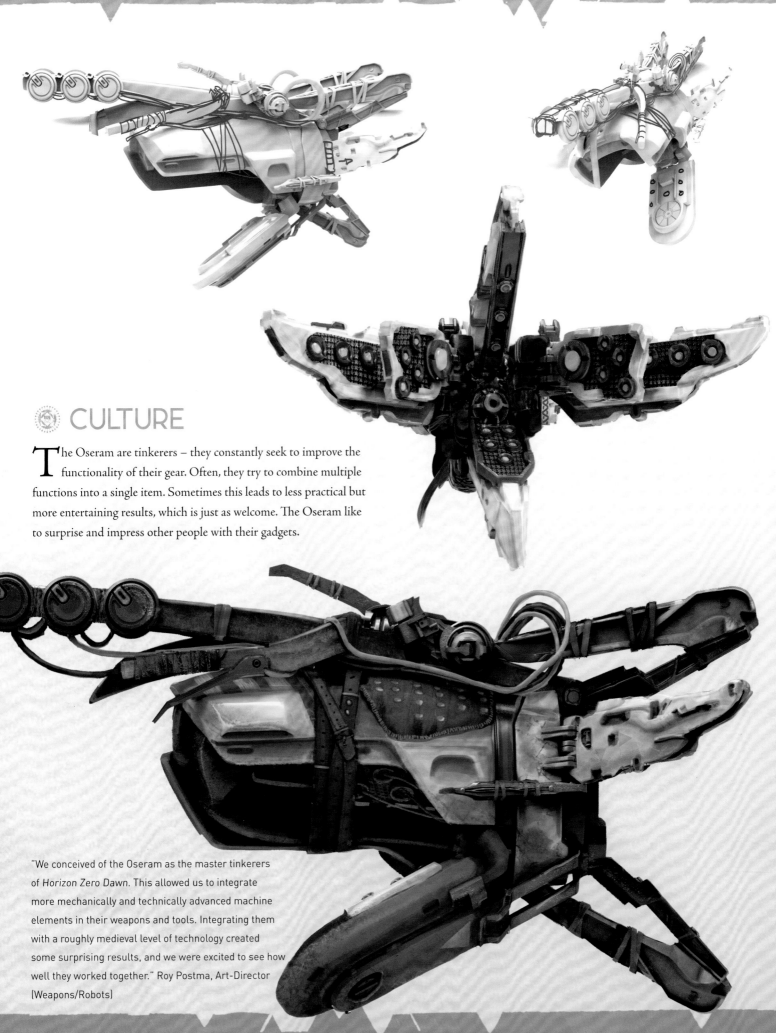

CULTURE

The Oseram are tinkerers – they constantly seek to improve the functionality of their gear. Often, they try to combine multiple functions into a single item. Sometimes this leads to less practical but more entertaining results, which is just as welcome. The Oseram like to surprise and impress other people with their gadgets.

"We conceived of the Oseram as the master tinkerers of *Horizon Zero Dawn*. This allowed us to integrate more mechanically and technically advanced machine elements in their weapons and tools. Integrating them with a roughly medieval level of technology created some surprising results, and we were excited to see how well they worked together." Roy Postma, Art-Director (Weapons/Robots)

ABOVE: The Oseram use metal anchors to clasp stone building blocks in place. Though the cultural preference is for simplicity, clever designs suggest pride in their work. Even something as low-key as this can color a player's perception of the village and its people.

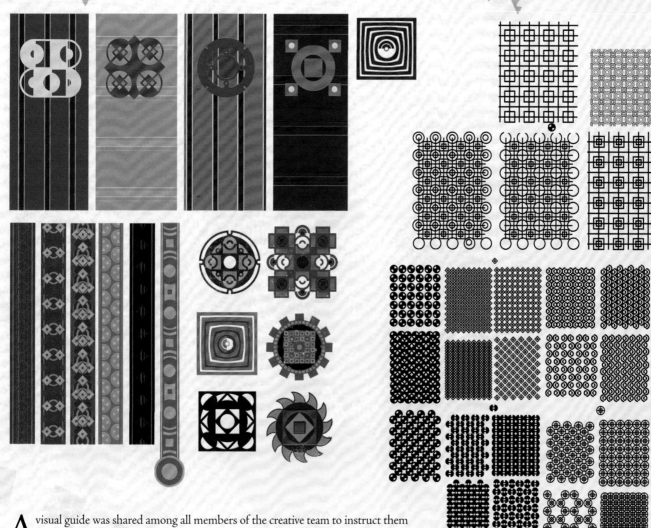

A visual guide was shared among all members of the creative team to instruct them on the 'Oseramification' of different objects and structures. Regardless of whether the job entailed designing props like mechanical hammers, or locking down elements of tribal motifs, the visual guide would ensure that it belonged in the Oseram culture. The mechanical hammer in question would have to show wear and tear, for example, to imply hardiness even after heavy usage. Basic weapons have a certain flair to their design, hinting at the intelligence behind the gruff Oseram façade. Icons are said to be heraldic, after a history of warring clans requiring identification. Non-heraldic designs are composed almost entirely of circles and squares.

BANDITS

Bandits are parasites, feeding off the endeavors of fellow survivors. They have no honor, but they do not entirely lack intelligence. Rather than produce anything themselves they raid villages and encampments, looting or sometimes claiming abandoned habitats entirely. Bandit sites comprise of improvised awnings and tents from numerous regions, some of which were grandiose but soon degraded. Bandit activity, in terms of concept, is intended to be filthy and ugly.

The anarchic Bandits transform almost everything into an irregular mishmash of incongruous material and form. Their main expertise, if it can be called that, is to repurpose loot in ways that are invariably terrifying: prisoner cages, weaponized alarm systems, or simply the degraded remnants of a once homely and inviting estate. An erratic bandit skyline is usually enough to ward off other tribes, and if that's not enough their crude graffiti will clearly communicate a hostile and animalistic intent.

A Nora house, claimed by Bandits. We do not know what became of the original occupants, but their battle was lost however it was fought.

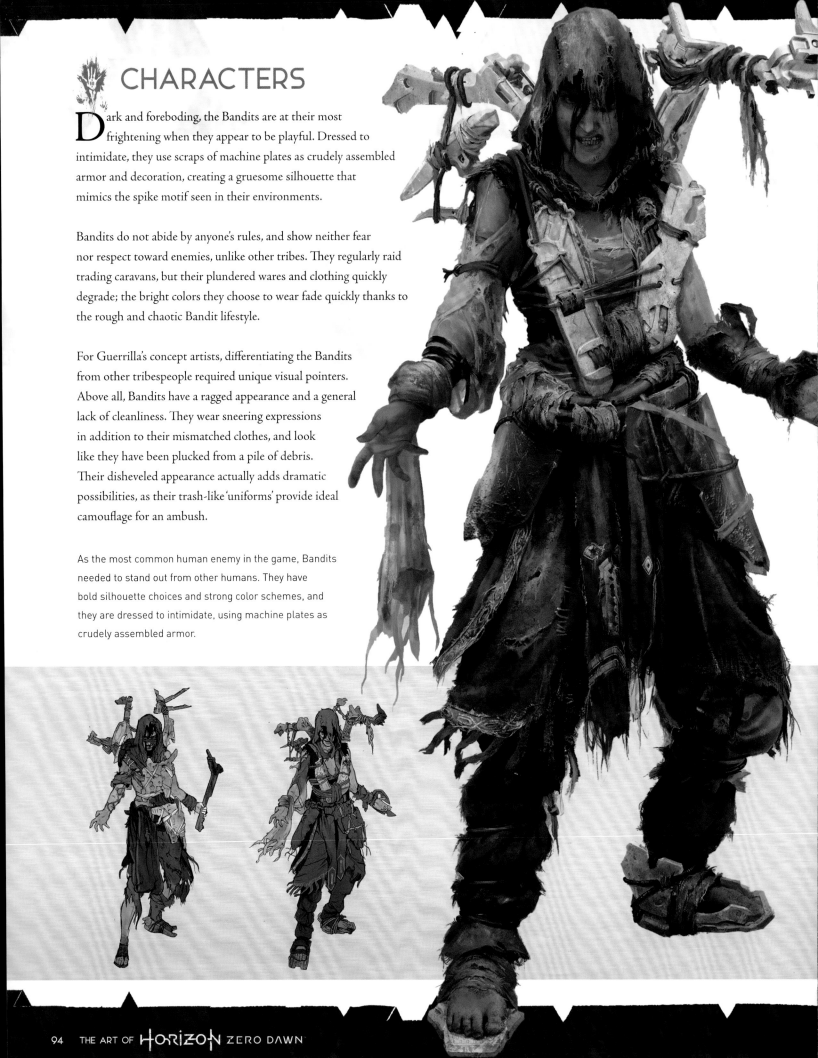

CHARACTERS

Dark and foreboding, the Bandits are at their most frightening when they appear to be playful. Dressed to intimidate, they use scraps of machine plates as crudely assembled armor and decoration, creating a gruesome silhouette that mimics the spike motif seen in their environments.

Bandits do not abide by anyone's rules, and show neither fear nor respect toward enemies, unlike other tribes. They regularly raid trading caravans, but their plundered wares and clothing quickly degrade; the bright colors they choose to wear fade quickly thanks to the rough and chaotic Bandit lifestyle.

For Guerrilla's concept artists, differentiating the Bandits from other tribespeople required unique visual pointers. Above all, Bandits have a ragged appearance and a general lack of cleanliness. They wear sneering expressions in addition to their mismatched clothes, and look like they have been plucked from a pile of debris. Their disheveled appearance actually adds dramatic possibilities, as their trash-like 'uniforms' provide ideal camouflage for an ambush.

As the most common human enemy in the game, Bandits needed to stand out from other humans. They have bold silhouette choices and strong color schemes, and they are dressed to intimidate, using machine plates as crudely assembled armor.

Bandit hierarchy is built on a simple principle: the strongest and meanest are in the top class, the rest are insignificant. Strong and tough Bandits deliver deadly ranged fire, while their crazed henchmen fight in close quarters.

LOCATIONS

In describing the Bandit influence on the land, Guerrilla's artistic leads refer to them as an 'infection'. Verdant landscapes and thriving villages are laid waste, starting a transformation process that involves slapdash restructuring and chaotic outfitting. Bandits are the plague of the land, and players will recognize their presence without having it spelled out for them.

Bandit intimidation tactics work extremely well against other tribes. In the approach to a Bandit refuge, monstrous totems are erected to dishearten outsiders. The totems, according to Guerrilla, are considered scarecrows that keep intruders away from camps. Occasionally, they are erected to frighten prisoners inside the camps.

INSET: By daylight, Bandit encampments are slightly less threatening, though they still retain their horrid appearance.

The concept artists chose a looser visual style to describe haphazard Bandit methodology. There are crisscrossed ramparts, precarious walkways and unkempt living quarters. In the foreground, hanging above the courtyard, we see a prisoner's cage – a figure of ridicule, which also points to the Bandits' tendency toward cruelty. The Bandits represent humanity at its lowest ebb. By nature, Bandits are an opportunistic rabble that lives in a state of chaos. This is also their primary weakness when facing tribes that are better organized and structured.

FAR LEFT: Bandit raiders return from a successful raid, boasting loot that appears to have been rustled from the Banuk. Pretty much everything now in their possession has been acquired by unscrupulous means, a situation that Aloy soon intends to put right.

Captured machines are rounded up and butchered – the sadistic entertainment factor counts at least as much as the desire to gain raw materials from the mechanical beasts, which the Bandits use to fortify their camps.

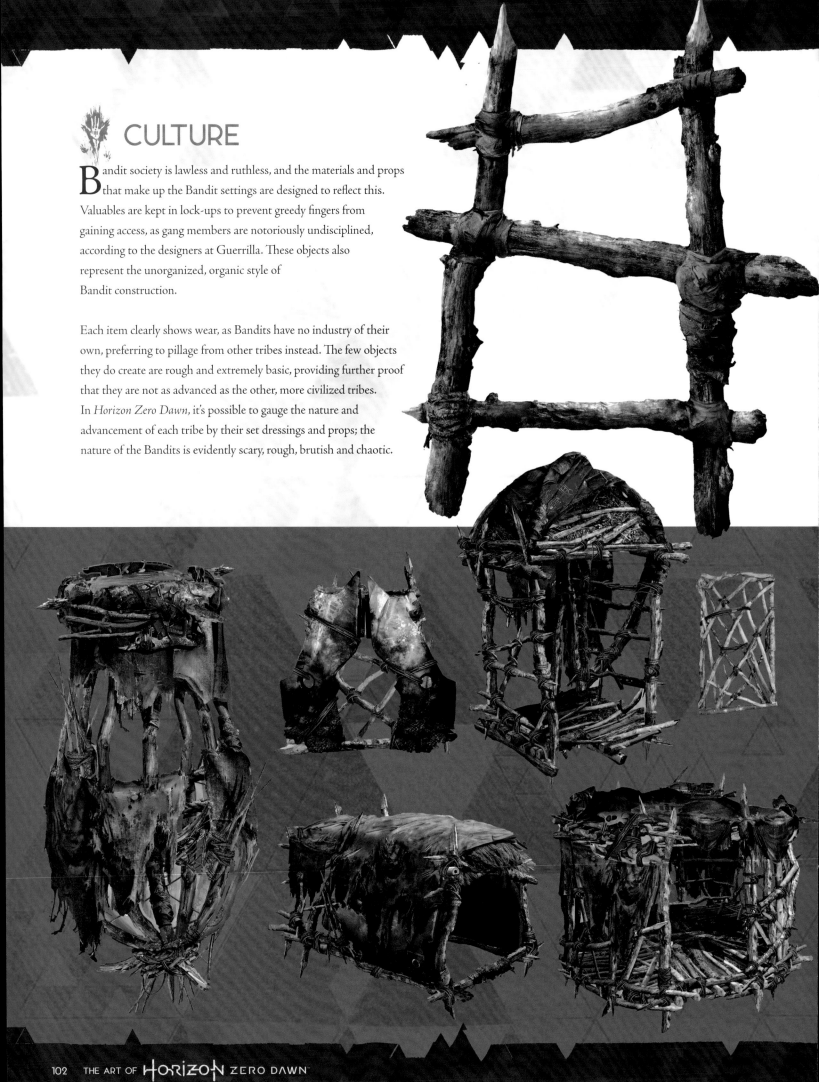

CULTURE

Bandit society is lawless and ruthless, and the materials and props that make up the Bandit settings are designed to reflect this. Valuables are kept in lock-ups to prevent greedy fingers from gaining access, as gang members are notoriously undisciplined, according to the designers at Guerrilla. These objects also represent the unorganized, organic style of Bandit construction.

Each item clearly shows wear, as Bandits have no industry of their own, preferring to pillage from other tribes instead. The few objects they do create are rough and extremely basic, providing further proof that they are not as advanced as the other, more civilized tribes. In *Horizon Zero Dawn*, it's possible to gauge the nature and advancement of each tribe by their set dressings and props; the nature of the Bandits is evidently scary, rough, brutish and chaotic.

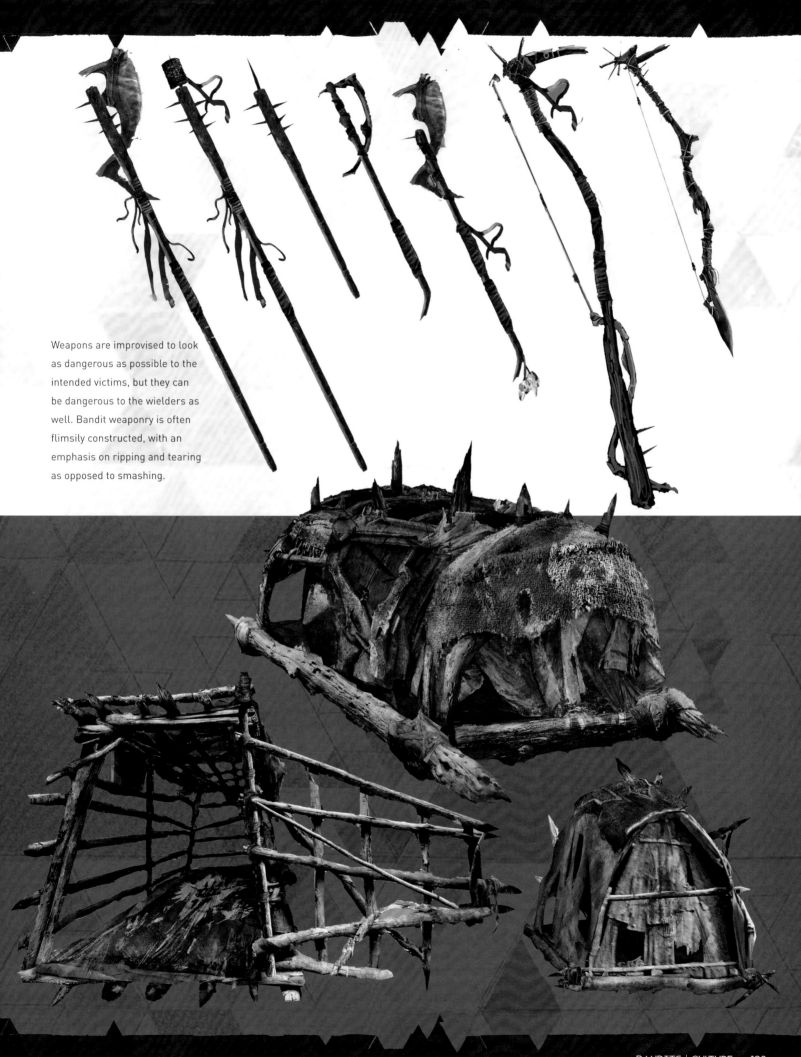

Weapons are improvised to look as dangerous as possible to the intended victims, but they can be dangerous to the wielders as well. Bandit weaponry is often flimsily constructed, with an emphasis on ripping and tearing as opposed to smashing.

TRIBES
BANUK

The Banuk are a nomadic northern tribe from the isolated boreal territory called Ban-Ur. As a culture based on the primacy of the hunt, the Banuk are fiercely individualistic. They see survival as a lonely imperative, a measure of the individual's will against the harsh extremes of their territory. That said, they do have some primitive but egalitarian social structures in place that enable their people to work together in a dangerous environment. The main political unit is the Werak, a unique Banuk concept that translates to something like 'pride' or 'troop'. A Werak is made up of families that band together to hunt. It is an extremely informal arrangement with few strictures – basically just a group of people that follow a superior hunter, who leads by example. Traditionally, the Chief is aided by a Shaman, whose job is to communicate with spirits that the Banuk believe reside in machines.

The nomadic nature of the Banuk is immediately apparent in this nighttime view of an encampment. Fires glowing within as chill winds blow outside may be analogous to the Banuk people's indomitable spirit. Tent profiles mirror the mountain peaks in the distance.

△ CHARACTERS

The Banuk are skilled warriors but even better hunters. The spear is their weapon of choice, and they obsess about finding sharper points (frequently from filing machine parts) and crafting stronger, more decorative shafts. They are particularly skilled at using spears to hit junctures between machine armor plates, damaging or incapacitating their prey.

The Banuk believe that machines are inhabited by benevolent spirits. It is not, however, taboo to hunt machines – on the contrary, a successful machine hunt proves that the benevolent spirit is rendering aid to the tribe with gifts of metal. Banuk Shamans are responsible for communicating with these spirits, and such rites have many purposes, including prayer, blessing, giving thanks, and asking for aid in the passage of souls to the afterlife.

"In the Banuk Shaman designs, I wanted to show the tribe's spiritual attitude towards machines. Huge head pieces created out of machine parts, shrouds of entangled cables and ribbons, incisions of robot cords that cover their hands – all to present them as beings between the human world and the machine world, capable of communicating with machines." Ilya Golitsyn

200 cm

150 cm

100 cm

50 cm

The individual's will to survive is the key tenet of Banuk life. A Banuk always strives to prove his or her worth, and there is great satisfaction in being the best hunter, the best fighter, the best guide, the best climber, or even the best at starting fires. Someone who combines all of these skills into a rugged, heroic survivalist is considered a paragon. There is no formal training for hunters and warriors; young men and women learn by watching and doing, usually from their parents. Everything is sink-or-swim: A true Banuk is honed by the ordeal of survival, and if they don't cut it, others will look to someone who can. The best hunter leads, male or female, and the other hunters are expected to acknowledge that their skills are inferior unless they can prove otherwise.

"Developing the Banuk was a chance to go a bit more tribal, compared to the aesthetics of the Nora and Carja people we'd done before. I wanted them to be the tribe that mimics the machines, since they almost live in harmony with the machines. Being the most colorful guy in the office, I made sure the Banuk also became the most colorful tribe in the game. It's a nice contrast to the more subdued color scheme of the Nora or the Oseram." Luc de Haan, Concept Artist

LOCATIONS

Banuk territory is truly unique, owing to how the people have claimed it. Rock formations are not crumbled – instead they are canvassed with color. Dense atmospheric conditions, notably geothermal mists, are convenient theatrical devices for Guerrilla to draw upon. The vast, basin-like composition of rugged plains surrounded by mountains suggests to players that tough challenges lie ahead, lurking behind the rocks and hiding inside forests.

The Banuk adopted one of the most inhospitable regions to make their first settlements, in the southern plains of the Yellowstone glacier. Detailed photography of the region as it exists in our time was highlighted by Guerrilla's concept artists as both dangerous and beautiful. The Banuk heartland appears as a resource-rich, mystical environment. Its geothermal properties inspire all the rich color schemes for Banuk Shaman artists. Monolithic natural formations are decorated with bright symbols that serve as landmarks.

CULTURE

"This image was made to give you a feeling of what daily life is like for a Banuk hunter. The struggle for heat, a captured machine ready to be transported to the camp, domesticated machines that help in the hunt, dressed up to the need of the hunter. This is a very early concept of a Banuk scene, where we suggest they have the ability to ride on machines. Later on it was removed, and machine riding was limited to Aloy. Still, among all the tribes of *Horizon Zero Dawn*, they are the closest to gaining any sort of control over machines, though they move in this direction almost blindfolded, through sheer trial and error." Luc de Haan.

A key role of the Shaman is divination – asking the machine spirits to help locate organic game or good machine hunting. Clever Shamans employ tricks to help with this task, possibly noting that the presence of a certain machine signifies a herd is near, or perhaps simply recognizing which hunters have a knack for tracking, then anointing them with spiritual honorifics. Still, over generations of closely observing the machines, the Banuk have learned much about their behavior.

ABOVE: "The Banuk tribe believes they have a spiritual connection with nature (the machines being part of it in their world) and express this in many aspects of their culture. They decorate themselves with parts and fluids harvested from their hunts, decorating not only their clothes and bodies, but also their surroundings." Lloyd Allan

LEFT: As nomads, the Banuk have few permanent structures, though they have been known to construct shelters and outposts from the metal skeletons of huge machines brought down by their hunters. Such places consist of little more than communal sleeping rooms and watering holes.

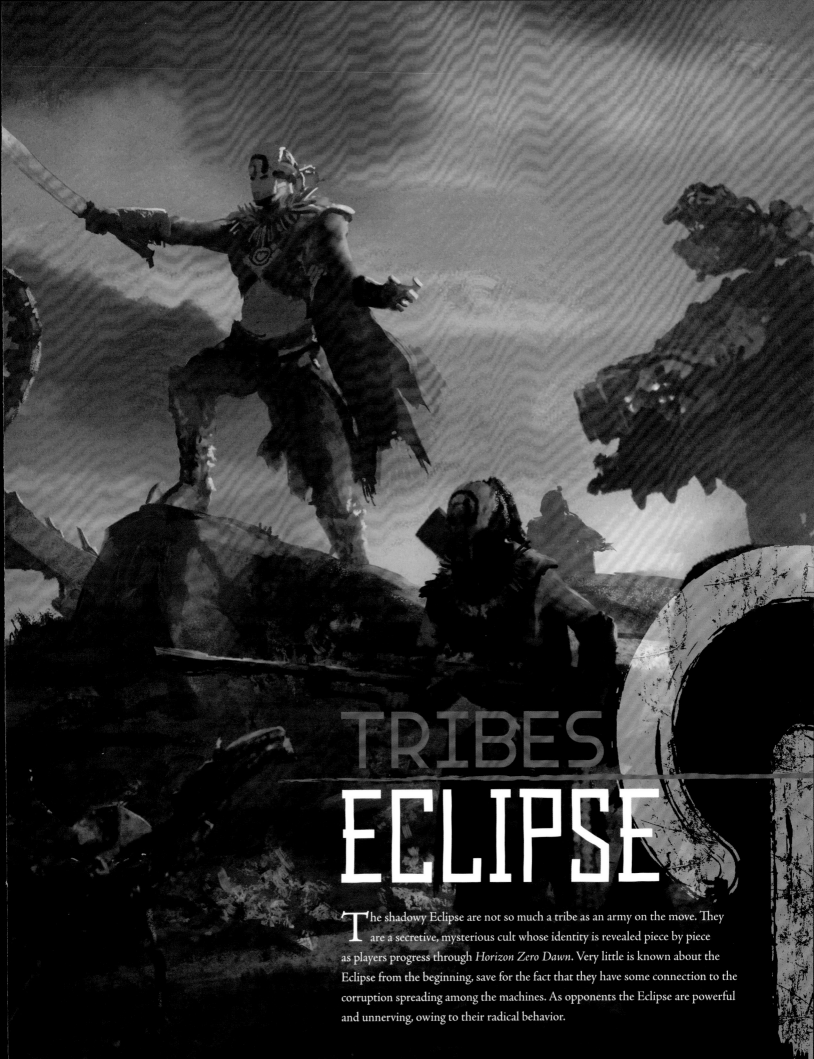

TRIBES

ECLIPSE

The shadowy Eclipse are not so much a tribe as an army on the move. They are a secretive, mysterious cult whose identity is revealed piece by piece as players progress through *Horizon Zero Dawn*. Very little is known about the Eclipse from the beginning, save for the fact that they have some connection to the corruption spreading among the machines. As opponents the Eclipse are powerful and unnerving, owing to their radical behavior.

The Eclipse soldiers dress ceremoniously to give a mystical impression. Their foes are intended to tremble at the sight of such strong and determined warriors. Many of their number are famed for their individual exploits, and are encouraged to adopt distinctive attire on the battlefield. This warlike motif appears in the use of ejected bullet casings from ancient war machines, which they work into totems and rosaries, as well as their masks, which they used to hide their identity.

"From the very early designs, we wanted to have a recognizable symbol from our everyday life become something special in the world of *Horizon Zero Dawn*. The power logo turned out to be a perfect match – it is simple and recognizable, it can be interpreted as a symbol of electronic resurrection, and thus associated with power over the machines or, ultimately, over life and death." Luc de Haan

"The Eclipse are a group of religious fanatics that are excavating ancient war machines to use for their own purposes. The challenge was to reflect this description in their designs, while also making sure that their outfits, buildings and artifacts were sufficiently different from those of other tribes. It seemed fitting to make the Eclipse structures rectangular, feeble and constructed in a rush, while also incorporating some of the bounties they dig up." Erik van Helvoirt, Concept Artist

Dark, brooding skies and flaming torches create an uncomfortable and dangerous atmosphere in this scene. One would expect to find Aloy sneaking around stealthily in the shadows, choosing her opportunities wisely.

RIGHT: "I wanted to create an image that portrays how powerful the Eclipse's leader is – not because of his own physique but rather because of what he controls: the destructive power of the ancient war machines." Luc de Haan

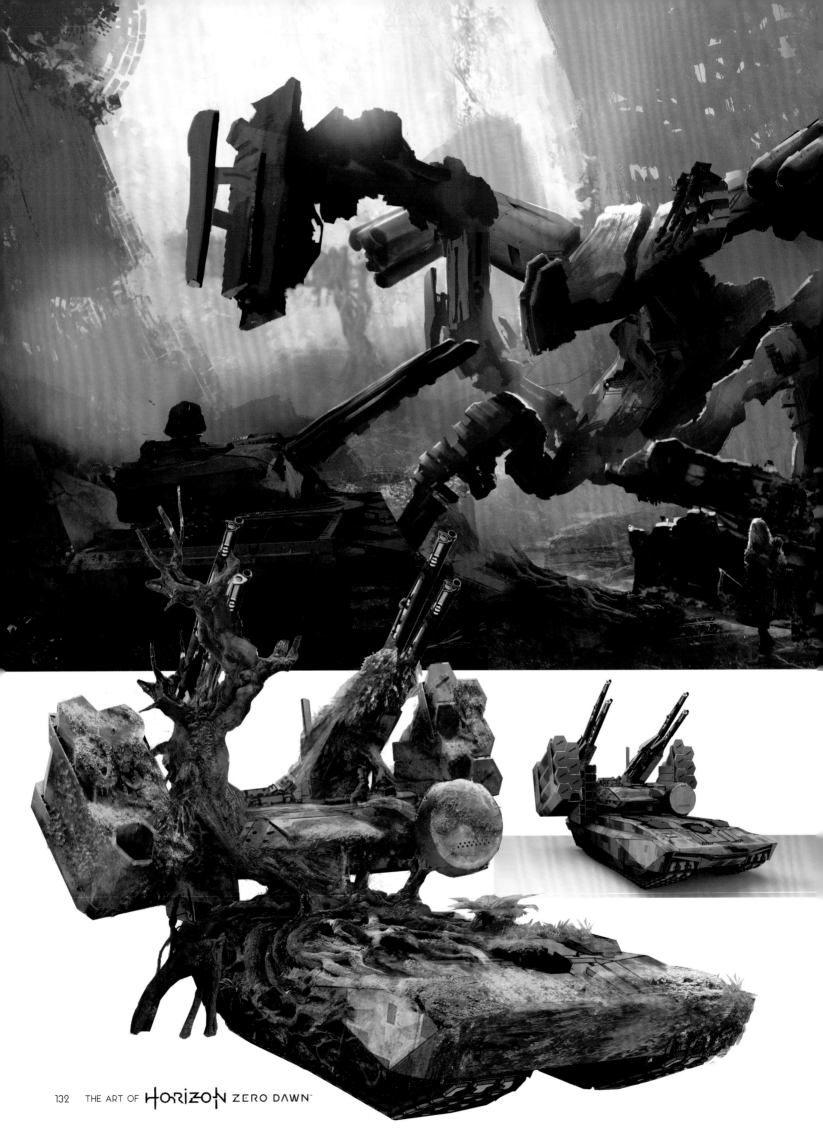

⚲ WAR MACHINES

The Eclipse have turned to excavating old war machines for their destructive abilities. The designs for the war machines are very non-organic, putting them at odds with other machines. They are also used as a visual device, to emphasize the stark contrast with the natural world in all its glory. The war machines seem to have been around before the end of the world – it's possible they even had a part in it…

Ancient military hardware lies dormant on the spot where it was last immobilized. Its occupants vanished long ago, their remains crumbled into dust and blown by the wind. But old intentions continue to stir somewhere in the land, urging Aloy to exercise caution.

"After working on our fauna-oriented organic machines, it was a fresh challenge to take a step back and think about our approach to the design of the war machines. We brought them back to the technology level and design aesthetics of our current era, and then augmented them to something people haven't seen before, capturing their raw power and destructive nature. This created a natural contrast between both machine factions." Roy Postma

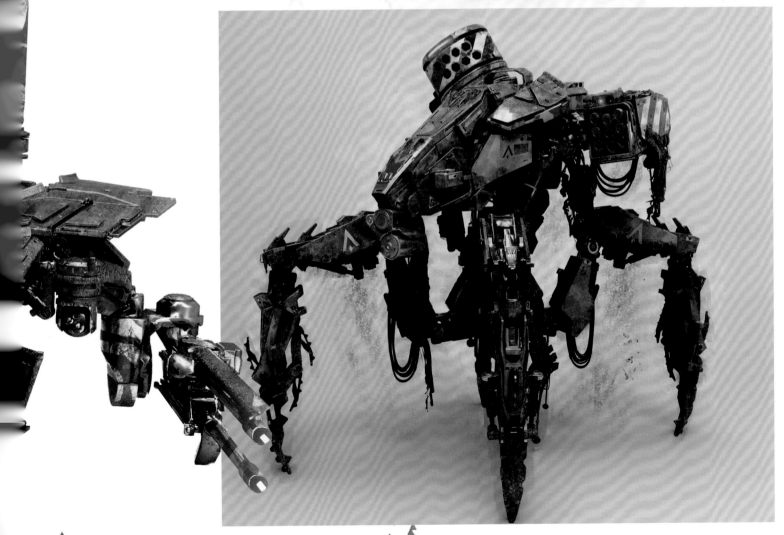

CREATURES
MACHINES

⊙ THE MACHINES

A significant part of the mystery that Aloy needs to solve in *Horizon Zero Dawn* is the origin of the machines. Their creation and purpose are only explained towards the end of the game, but it's clear from the outset that they've been roaming around for much longer than the tribes. Just like animals, machines are sentient creatures with their own ecosystem. No single machine type can function outside of this system; each type has its own role to fulfill, and it needs the other types to survive.

To reflect this naturalistic approach, Guerrilla tried to have as many machines work and relate together as possible. The artists were quick to adopt highly optimized shapes and forms for the machines, to suggest different roles and functions for each type. Other aspects of the machine designs took longer to crystalize, as a delicate balance needed to be struck between organic shapes and advanced mechanical elements.

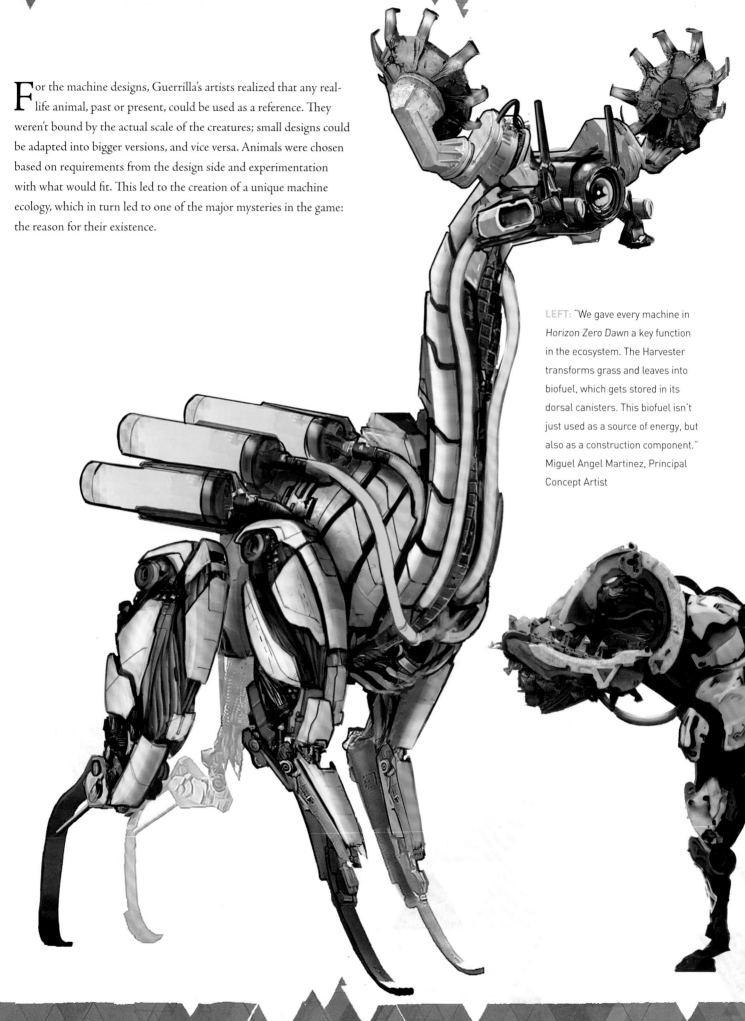

For the machine designs, Guerrilla's artists realized that any real-life animal, past or present, could be used as a reference. They weren't bound by the actual scale of the creatures; small designs could be adapted into bigger versions, and vice versa. Animals were chosen based on requirements from the design side and experimentation with what would fit. This led to the creation of a unique machine ecology, which in turn led to one of the major mysteries in the game: the reason for their existence.

LEFT: "We gave every machine in *Horizon Zero Dawn* a key function in the ecosystem. The Harvester transforms grass and leaves into biofuel, which gets stored in its dorsal canisters. This biofuel isn't just used as a source of energy, but also as a construction component." Miguel Angel Martinez, Principal Concept Artist

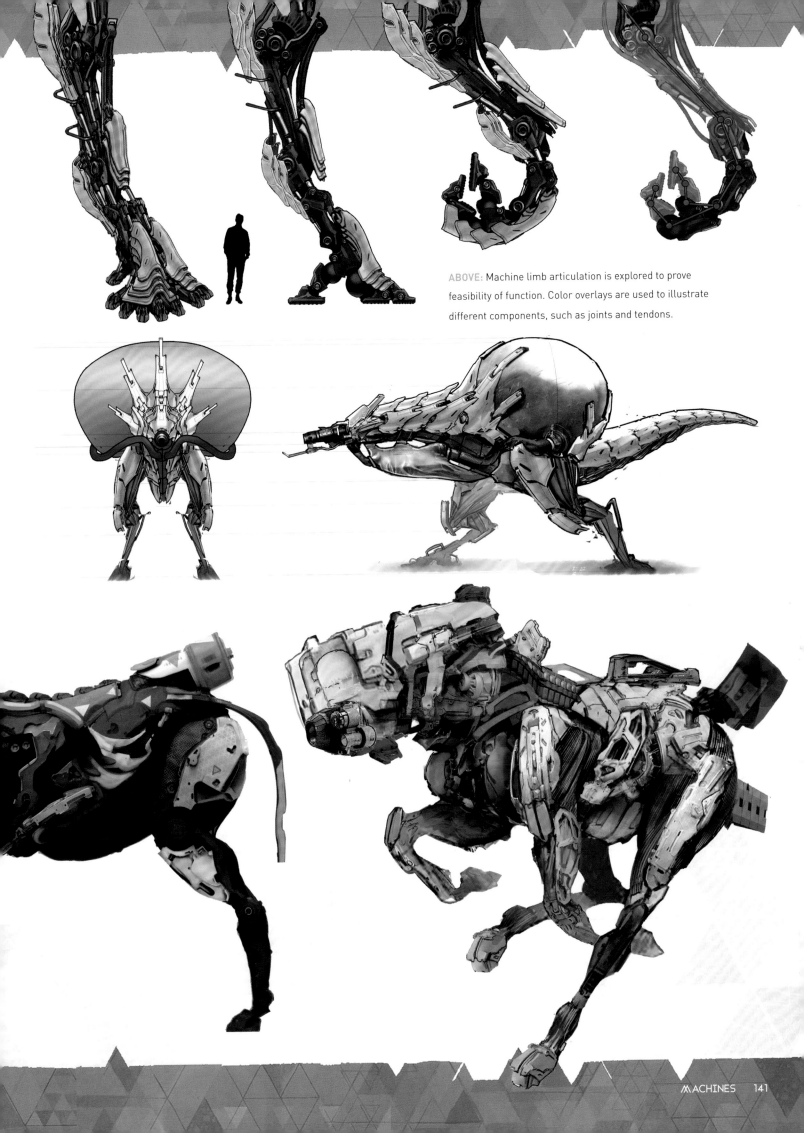

ABOVE: Machine limb articulation is explored to prove feasibility of function. Color overlays are used to illustrate different components, such as joints and tendons.

The machines form an ecosystem and work together towards a common goal. Players will notice how each type of machine has its own role to play, such as defense, harvesting/resource gathering, communications, transportation, and even cleaning up. Guerrilla has portrayed a vision of a self-sustaining system that aims to recondition the Earth – something vastly complex and fascinating to observe.

MACHINE ESSENCE

One of the strongest design decisions in the development of the machines was the adoption of carnivore and herbivore traits. Aggressive machine types were contrasted with more docile ones, the latter becoming involved with tasks like harvesting and transportation. This distinction also helped players to gauge whether their prey would attack on sight or attempt to flee.

In the concept below, the machines look right at home. If it weren't for the unusual lights and head shapes, one would almost need a second look to distinguish the machines from their natural counterparts.

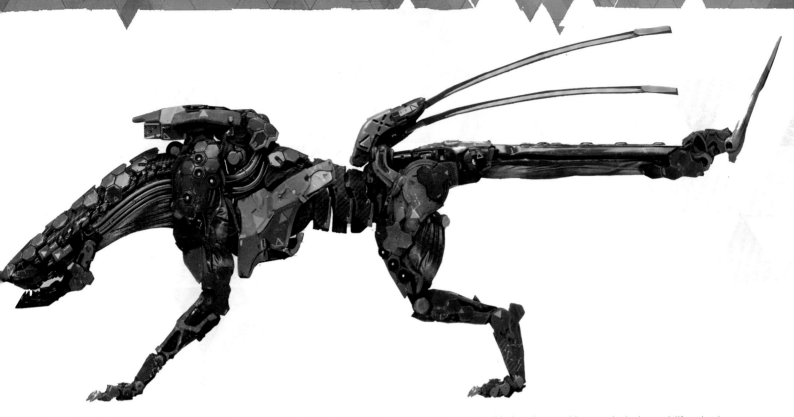

ABOVE: "The Stalker is an ambush predator that uses cloaking and traps to catch its prey off-guard. As with the other machines, we looked at real-life animals and tried to incorporate their characteristics into the design. In this case, the base is formed by the maned wolf – it has long legs that make it seem very fast and agile. The hexagonal plating on the side acts as a cloaking device, and gives it a high-tech look." Erik van Helvoirt

⊙ FORM AND FUNCTION

In designing the Tallneck, one of the toughest challenges was to come up with a purpose for its graceful aesthetic. Essentially an enormous, mobile focus point for the player, the Tallneck requires a lot of space to move around it. This makes the machine less suitable to certain environments. As such, it took a while for the idea of the Tallneck to 'click'. The initial concept was well-liked, but finalizing it required approval from a lot of different stakeholders, who all had different demands and restrictions for the machine.

A single sketch drove the concept of the Tallneck, which has been through many iterations since that earliest design. The core idea of a communication disc replacing the head of a giraffe has stuck with the concept that is still in the game. Its image is now iconic, impossible to separate from *Horizon Zero Dawn*.

Top view

Bottom view

Use same materials and textures for bottom as the top of the wing flaps

"When we designed the Stormbird, we wanted to give the majesty and power of an eagle to an advanced defensive machine. Built to protect the transport machines from external threats, it is able to condense static electricity from the air into defensive lighting, which stuns and damages its enemies." Miguel Angel Martinez

⊙ FIRST CONCEPTS

When work on the machines started, the link to real-life animals was quickly made. However, it took a while for the team to reach the point where every design was based on more natural, organic shapes. The artists tried to avoid typical human engineering cues, like mathematical shapes.

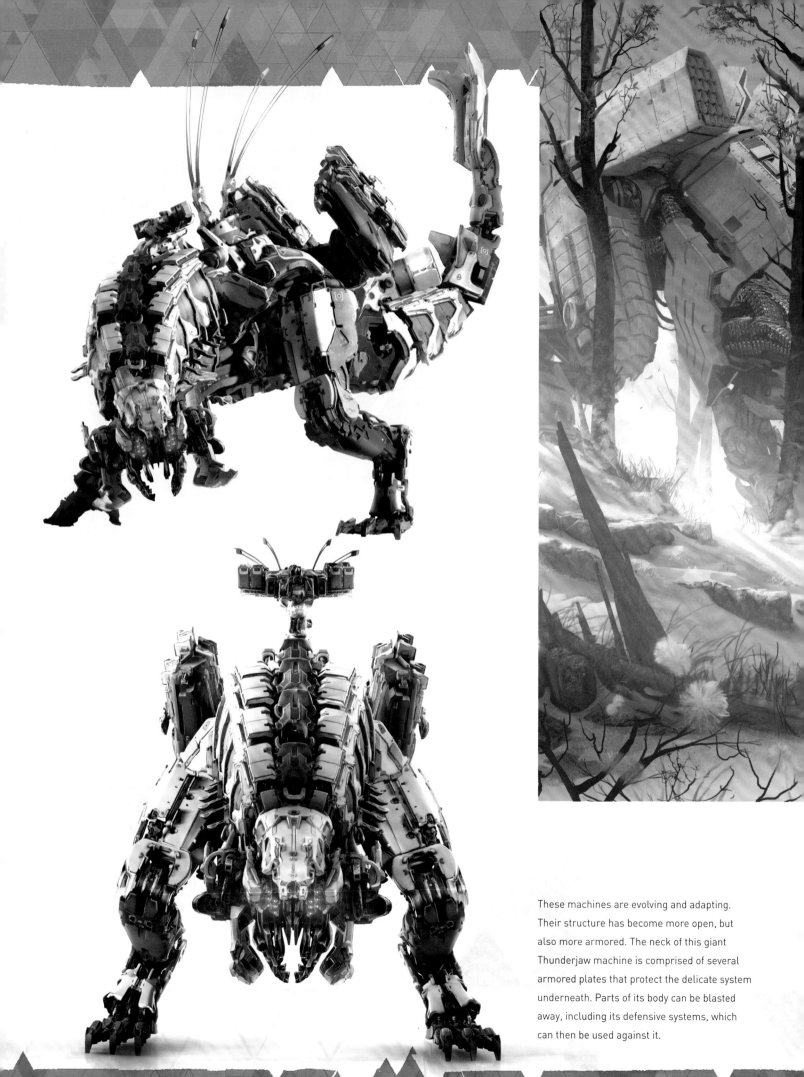

These machines are evolving and adapting. Their structure has become more open, but also more armored. The neck of this giant Thunderjaw machine is comprised of several armored plates that protect the delicate system underneath. Parts of its body can be blasted away, including its defensive systems, which can then be used against it.

⊙ FACTS BEHIND THE FICTION

To inform the authenticity of the designs, Guerrilla's visual art and story teams consulted with a robotics professor. They talked extensively about how the machines would be produced from a technical perspective – whether they could be 3D-printed, and how that might allow for better integrated functionality, combining structural strength with a nervous system. Thinking along organic lines drove the team back to the drawing board, where they reconstructed the machines with functional skeletal systems.

SECRET LIVES OF MACHINES

It took a while for Guerrilla to settle on a specific look that worked for all machines. The Watcher, for instance, went through one of the longest design trajectories of any machine in *Horizon Zero Dawn*. Initially based on a small bipedal dinosaur, his appearance kept changing and evolving throughout the project. However, there was a sense of personality in the appearance, poses and movements of the Watcher that made him a team favorite. Unsurprisingly, the machines that made it into the final game all had similarly recognizable personalities.

The exaggerated shapes on the machines hint at their core functionality. For example, the Watcher has a big central 'eye' because it is a machine built for surveillance and scanning, and this needs to be clearly communicated to the player. In this concept art, machines are surveying the forest.

RUINS

As mysterious and awe-inspiring as the ancient cities of the past, this is what our cities could look like 1000 years from today. When Aloy enters the world of her forebears, it is no less breathtaking than expected. Gazing upon these structures with her own eyes for the first time, she realizes that there is truth to the stories her people tell about the Old Ones. From afar the ruins appear majestic, though the towers resemble nothing so much as epitaphs to a dead civilization. They have a magnetic hold on Aloy's curiosity, and players are compelled to investigate along with her.

Though nature laid a blanket over the remains, laying the Old Ones to rest, the secret of the machines still stirs somewhere within. Beneath towers so tall they disappear into clouds, Aloy will have her answers revealed. She would stop and marvel at this fateful moment, but the silence of the lost city has an unnerving effect.

DESOLATION

With the natural landscape obscured from view, all that lays before Aloy now is ruins. Resting below an ossified traffic light stand – its concept entirely alien to her – the city appears as a jungle of crumbling facades. This place is no longer welcoming, but foreboding; it feels forgotten and thrown away. Above all, it presents a challenge to Aloy, which is a central theme to *Horizon Zero Dawn*. Familiar skills learned while navigating her homeland must now be adapted, and she must be on her guard.

However, there is also the sense of a new day dawning – and with it, an air of discovery. There is hope amid the rubble, and a sense of excitement over the possible avenues of exploration.

INSET: Anyone with a sense of adventure will wish to dive straight into such a scene. One can almost imagine the chill from the water, adding to the coolness of the morning air. These ruins may be among Aloy's first sightings of the Old Ones. She is on the right trail.

BELOW: Aloy stands alone in what might once have been a busy thoroughfare, the overgrown setting a far cry from the bustle of burger stands, ticket booths and fast food restaurants. She would have no concept of this, and we are encouraged to leave such imagery behind.

BELOW: Swooping, reclaimed terrain hides the angular structures that once were. There's an oversized donut atop one building, which would have been jolly and comforting in its day. Consigned to the dim, distant past, our need to consume coffee and cake seems strange.

⚏ ORGANIC DEGRADATION

One of the problems with creating sci-fi imagery that's intended to look prehistoric, is that almost nothing has symmetry. Gazing upon something that's decrepit, we expect the unevenness; the broken, sagging and lopsided. Such models almost need to be sculpted, rather than mathematically rendered. Texture artists also face a colossal challenge to show the patchiness of the weather-worn effects. If the player spots repeated patterns, the illusion is broken. This is why such scenes are rarely attempted to the degree seen in *Horizon Zero Dawn*. Sorrowful shapes are deliberately imposed on the structures, while light and shadow are used to describe detail in sepulchral hues. It all appears chillingly real.

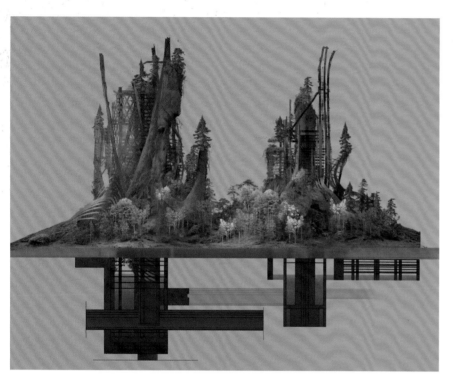

A cross section of the ancient city reveals mysterious structures below.

Stairways that reach to nowhere, and supports that have long since broken down. Frailty is evident throughout these concepts, evoking pity for those that once felt so comfortable and safe among these structures. As daylight streams through the window frames and reveals sections of collapsed wall, it almost seems like the trees that surround these broken building have come to pay their final respects.

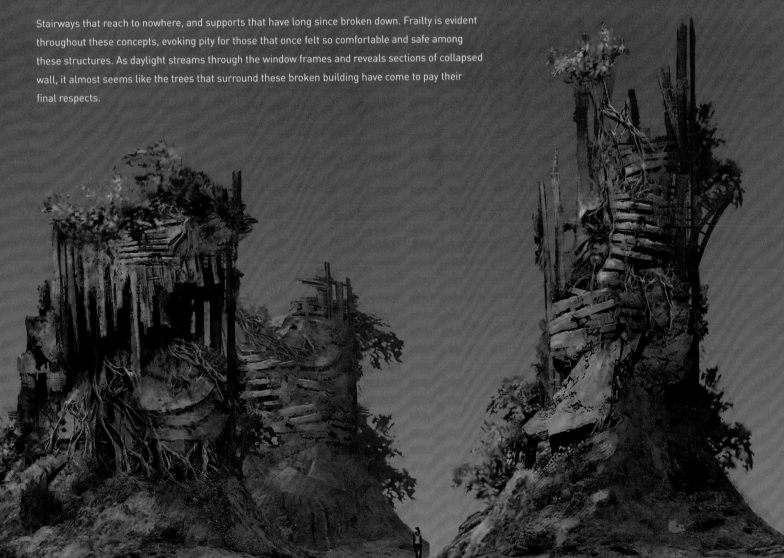

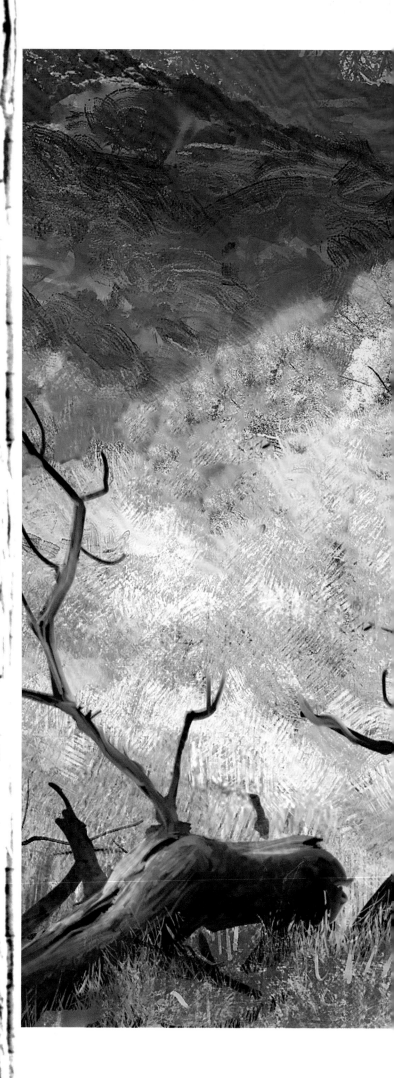

An example of the thoroughness with which concepts are explored. A town is shown in various stages of decay and gradual reclamation. Its lines become softened by nature until most of them vanish.

Living waters and an imagined hillside breeze make this scene
feel refreshing, like it was intended for players to breathe in
its beauty. Much like gameplay pacing and story pacing, visual
pacing is important to keep an adventurous spirit alive and
eager to face the next challenge.

"We designed different vehicles and drones for our pre-apocalyptic vision of the future. These are now rusted wrecks scattered throughout the world, giving the players a glimpse of the futuristic things that are now in Aloy's past." Lloyd Allan

THE CAULDRONS

A loy stands inside an immense machine foundry crackling with power. This place is not intended for humans; the machines do not need warmth and they may not even require the light. The Cauldrons are the embodiment of function over form, though the anatomical nature of the machine birth sites reveals some traces of manmade structure. Navigation will be difficult for Aloy with few, if any, clues as to which surfaces are safe to tread or touch. This alien environment presents a challenge for which she is unprepared. Players are shown where to go, but not how to go, relying on a kind of gut instinct informed by Aloy's exploits in previous areas.

The Cauldrons are fully automated; their workings have remained a mystery to the tribes for hundreds of years.

"While designing the Cauldrons, we came up with the idea to have the machines cut away rock using a triangular laser and build a cavern resembling an ant colony. Since the robots are part of a cycle of life on the surface of the planet, it was important to make the Cauldron feel like a living organism."
Erik van Helvoirt

Two concepts explore the same scene under different lighting conditions, helping the design team to decide which is better suited to first sightings of the Cauldron. With a triangular threshold in the rock and a procession of smaller robots, there's something unusual happening here.

BUNKERS

These underground complexes are isolated and relatively well-preserved pockets of the old world, representing the last hiding places of humans before doomsday. It's also where Aloy finds more clues about the fate of the Old Ones.

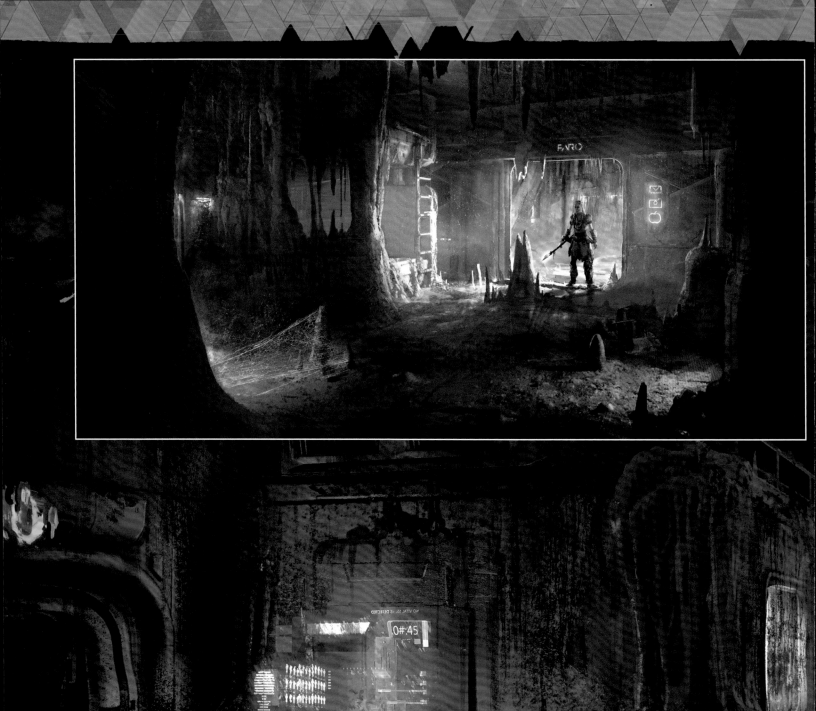

"The design process of the bunkers consisted of us first exploring what bunkers would look like in the future. During the second design phase we aged them, slowly blending them into natural caverns." Lloyd Allan

"Bunkers are strategic strongholds full of military equipment. When Aloy journeys into the bunkers to find answers, she crosses paths with the Eclipse, who are after the military hardware. This picture shows a military bunker punctured by a hostile war machine." Lloyd Allan

ACKNOWLEDGMENTS

The art in this book is created by Guerrilla's concept-art department and two external studios; Karakter and Sixmorevodka. Without their hard work and dedication, this book could not exist.

GUERRILLA

Art Directors Jan-Bart van Beek | Roy Postma | Dan Calvert | Alex Zapata | Maarten van der Gaag | Misja Baas | Arjan Bak

Concept Artists Lloyd Allan | Lois van Baarle |Richard Dumont | Eric Felten | Ilya Golitsyn | Luc de Haan | Erik Helvoirt | Kait Kybar | Miguel Angel Martinez | Joseph Noel | Jorry Rosman | Michel Voogt | Koen Wijffelaars | Miles Williams | Roland Ijzermans

Guerrilla Games Management: Hermen Hulst | Steven ter Heide | Angie Smets | Mathijs de Jonge | Michiel van der Leeuw | Lambert Wolterbeek Muller

Concept Art interns and temps Thomas Abna | Bob Albers | Robin Bouwmeester | Terrence Carter | Alanay Cekic | Charly Cheung | Yu Ting Chiu | Maurice Diemeer | Joris Dijkhuis | Scott Gravee | Suzanne Helmich | Rolandos Jankauskas | Daniel Joustra | Hakan Kamar | Matthias Kapuvari | Robert Kiss | Rutger Klunder | Isabella Koelman | Tom Kolbeek | Tino Kort | Guido Kuip | Malte Langheim | Chander Lieve | Stan Loiseaux | Yannick Maaskant | Ruben Matevosyan | Marinda Mensch | Chereton Mercelina | Jonas Minnebo | Danar Mohamed | Mike Andrew Nash | Lisa Plokker | Damir Popovic | Siim Rimm | Ramtin Saeedi | Adriaan Stam | Thomas Stoop | Samantha van der Touw | Willem van Lelyveld | Noud van Miltenburg | Eelco van Rooij | Inge van Schallenburg | Jort van Welbergen | Sander Verhoeven | Max Wedding | Ab Wienk | Danar Worya | Robin Wouters

Guerrilla Team: Elroy Aarts | Kim Aava | Nasier Abdoel | Isak Aberg Nordmark | Nikhat Ali | Daniele Antinolfi | Leo Arler | Sem Assink | Brian Baltus | Ana Barbuta | Denis Barth | Karim Baz | Jelle van der Beek | Richard van Beersum | Arjen Beij | Desmond van den Berg | Felix van den Bergh | Yvonne von Berg-Meijboom | Julian Berteling | Bas Bijpost | Stuart Billinghurst | Cesar Bittar | Tony Blokker | Lucas Bolt | Eric Boltjes | Oscar van den Bosch | Lucas Bramlage | Dennis van den Broek | Wim van Brussel | Gary Buchanan | Giliam de Carpentier | Fries Carton | Neil Chatterjee | Jonathan Colin| Frank Compagner | Lennart Denninger | Bernd Diemer | Andrius Drevinskas | Kenzo ter Elst | Benjamin Erdt | Joel Eschler | Jose Ayllon Escribano | Fenske Everhartz | Jan Jaap Fahner | Martin Felis | Niko Fernandez | David Ford | Jonny Frammington |Lennart Franken | Rigel Freeman | Julian Fries | Joshua van Gageldonk | Victor Gaza | Cayle George | Marijn Giesbertz | Angela Gillespie | Robin Gomar | Dave Gomes | John Gonzalez | Paul van Grinsven | | Niels de Groen | Stefan Groenewoud | Guido de Haan | Riem Halawani | Rob Heald | Jeroen Heemskerk | Kim van Heest | Emile van der Heide | Paul van der Heijden | Mas Hein | Sjoerd Hendriks | Anthonie van der Heul | Tim Hijkema | Trevor van Hoof | Paul-Jon Hughes | Alexander Hush | Ivana Ivakic | Olaf Jansen | Willem Janssen | Ben Jaramillo | Wouter Josemans | Hakan Kamar | Annika Kappner | Bryan Keiren | Pieter van de Kerkhof | Jacqueline Kerkmeijer | Björn Kjerrgren | Hylke Kleve | James Kneuper II | Oliver Kogelnig | Tom Kolbeek | Floris Kooij | Chaime Korper | Jeroen Krebbers | Thijs Kruithof | Midas de Laat | Francois Lacharriere | Stefan Lauwers | Perry Leijten | Peer Lemmers | Nick Liburd | Delano Lobman | Vladimir Lopatin | Hugh Malan | Troy Mashburn | Yannick Massa | Benjamin McCaw | Ronnie McFarlane | Joseph McKernan | David McMullen | Guy Michielsens | Klaas van der Molen | Robert Morcus | Jaap van der Muijden | Patrick Munnik | Florentina Neagu | Niek Neervens | Daniele Niero | Eva Nieuwdorp | Eri Noda | Riesh Varma Oedayrajsingh | Bo van Oord | Bart van Oosten | Wilbert Oosterom | Kevin Örtegren | Richard Oud | Edouard Peregrine | Hakan Persson | Johanna Persson | Mark Peters | Francisco Peters | Willy Pieper | Marco Pisanu | Kristal Plain | Blake Politeski | Kevin Quaid | Blake Rebouche | Stefan Reek | David Fornies Reyes | Jessica Riga | Brian Roberts | Jeroen Roding | Tommy de Roos | Mathijs Roosen | Carles Martinez Ros | Jorrit Rouwé | Adriaan de Ruijter | Ahmed Salama | Gilbert Sanders | Jelle van Scherpenzeel | Eelke Schipper | Arno Schmitz | Andrew Schneider | Samantha Schoonen | Ben Schrijvers | Ben Schroder | Katharina Schuetz | Bastian Seelbach | Samrat Sharma | Laurens Simonis | Andrew Simpson | Vincent van Soest | Espen Sogn | Igor Soldo | Ben Sprout | Jana Stadeler | Adriaan Stam | Sander van der Steen | Roderick van der Steen | Tim Stobo | Remco Straatman | Patrick Stroombergen | Dan Sumaili | Leszek Szczepanski | Jacob Tai | Pinar Temiz | Jamie Teo | Lucas van tol | Alina Ushakova | Andrea Varga | Berendine Venemans | Bryan Verboon | Sander Vereecken | Sander Verhoeven | Matthijs Verkuijlen | Tim Verweij | Tommy Visser | Tiffany Vongerichten | Michel Voogt | Leon Voorrips | Nathan Vos | Elco Vossers | Steven de Vries | Joeri Vromman | Nick Watkins | Kasper Wessing | Ryan Wetherall | Daniel Wewerinke | Anton Wiegert | Bart Weijsman | Sietske Wielsma | Jochen Willemsen | Marcel de Wit | Anton Woldhek | Cho Yan Wong | Tyler Woodburn | Jessica Wyeth | Anne van der Zanden | Dennis Zoetebier | Dennis Zopfi | Victor Zuylen

karakter
DESIGN STUDIO